MY TURN TO LEAD

Fundamentals of Leadership and Influence for New and Emerging Leaders

BY

Dr. Tonisha M. Pinckney

Contributing Author
Loretta L. Stevens

Photography: JawBorne Creations, LLC.
Cover Model: Morissa L. Stevens

Copyright Notice

Copyright © 2018 by Tonisha M. Pinckney, Ph.D.

ISBN: 978-0-578-21414-6

Cover Photography: ©2018 JawBorne Creations, LLC.
Cover Model: Morissa L. Stevens

DEDICATION

To all the leaders I have ever known
- better or worse –
I learned from you!

To my mother who taught me the importance of being a leading lady in the home, church, and community, while reminding me that leadership is about serving.

My sons, LDP & TJP, I love and appreciate you!
I am so proud of your leadership skills and potential!
You amaze me. #DopestDudesEver

I am also grateful to the many experts who contributed time and provided their expertise to help deliver a balanced perspective on leadership.

Contents

Preface...2

Chapter One: The Evolution of Leadership........................6

DEFINING LEADERSHIP..6

CHARACTERISTICS OF A LEADER 6

LEADERSHIP PRINCIPLES...7

A BRIEF HISTORY OF LEADERSHIP 9

THREE THEORIES OF LEADERSHIP..........................11

Advice for a U.S. Army Veteran: Kurt Schoenig...............16

Chapter Two: Context and Narrative 17

Three Mistakes of Bad Leaders: Lleuella Morris 20

Chapter Three: Situational Leadership...........................23

Situational Leadership: Telling..........................24

Situational Leadership: Selling 24

Situational Leadership: Participating 25

Situational Leadership: Delegating 25

Practical Illustration 26

Chapter Four: A Personal Inventory................................29

An Introduction to Kouzes and Posner 29

A PERSONAL INVENTORY.......................................30

Creating an Action Plan..*30*

Practical Illustration *31*

Self-Management and Core Competencies: Dr. Alexander Lowry
....*34*

Chapter Five: Inspiring a Shared Vision............................ **36**

Authenticity..*36*

Choosing Your Vision..*38*

Communicating Your Vision *38*

Identifying the Benefit for Others..*39*

Practical Illustration *39*

It's About Attitude: Sophie Miles..*42*

Chapter Six: Quality Leaders Produce Quality Leaders **43**

Determining Your Way..*43*

Being an Inspirational Role Model *44*

Influencing Others' Perspectives *44*

Practical Illustration *45*

Commitment to Developing and Empowering: Joanna Tropp-Bluestone..*47*

So, You Know You are a Bad Leader: Wayne Strickland..*49*

Chapter Seven: Innovative Leadership **51**

Think Outside the Box..*51*

Developing Your Inner Innovator *52*

Seeing Room for Improvement *53*

Lobbying for Change *54*

Maintaining control in a meeting *55*

Practical Illustration *58*

Chapter Eight: Empowering Others to Act **60**

Encouraging Growth in Others..........................*60*

Creating Mutual Respect..................................*61*

The Importance of Trust...................................*61*

Practical Illustration *62*

Have a 'Do Not Do List': Brian Liam *65*

Perspectives on Leadership: What Does It Take?............*65*

17 Traits of a Successful Leader: Wayne Strickland........*73*

Chapter Nine: Church Leadership by Pastor Loretta L. Stevens 75

CHURCH MEETINGS...*76*

DELEGATE..*76*

DEACONS/TRUSTEES/PASTORS ASSISTANTS...................*78*

RELATIONSHIPS *79*

CONCLUDING THOUGHTS *79*

Chapter Ten: Diversity with Inclusion **80**

Perspectives in Leadership: Women in Leadership *84*

Chapter Eleven: Encourage and Motivate Your Followers 94

Sharing Rewards..*94*

Celebrating Accomplishments...*95*

Making Celebration Part of Your Culture *95*

Practical Illustration *95*

Good Leadership is Not a Mystery: Dr. Joyce Mikal-Flynn98

Chapter Twelve: Influencing Your Followers................. 100

The Art of Persuasion *101*

The Principles of Influence..............................*101*

Practical Illustration *103*

No One Wants to be the 'Grim Reaper': Kristin Halpin Perry   106

No More Secret Squirrels: John Barker..........................*108*

Chapter Thirteen: Realistic and S.M.A.R.T. Goals.......... 110

Setting S.M.A.R.T. Goals 110

Creating a Long-Term (Strategic) Plan.......................111

Creating a Support System 111

Practical Illustration.................................112

Chapter Fourteen: The End is Just the Beginning.......... 115

References 117

About the Author 123

Preface

They say that leaders are born, not made. While it is true that some people are born leaders, some leaders are born in the midst of adversity. Some people become leaders when they see a need that must be filled. Those people who may have never had a leadership role stand up and take the lead when a situation requires it. Others, become leaders out of frustration with current leadership. More of the, "I can do it better," attitude. Does it matter? Not really

Why did you become a leader? Why do you want to lead? How do you know that you can lead? The point is that you are now a leader and you need to know how to lead. Not everyone has a mentor or access to their mentor. Not everyone has the luxury of learning how to lead before they are elevated to a leadership position. Some of you may be discouraged because people have yet to see your leadership potential. As you read this book, you will learn the techniques of true leadership and how to influence change while motivating your current or soon-to-be followers.

When I embarked on writing this book, I wanted to help readers build their confidence. Followers are like sharks in water that smell blood or animals that sense fear. Followers sense when leaders lack confidence in the power of their role, their ability to lead, or their vision. Of course, the more experience you have engaging others as a genuine leader, the easier it will be for you. It is never easy to take the lead, as you will need to make decisions and face challenges, but it can become natural and rewarding. There are may types of leaders and leadership styles. I can give you my opinion, but ultimately it is up to you (self-leadership) to decide which leadership and communication style suit your personality and the context in which you are leading or will lead.

Influence is subtle, yet incredibly powerful. You can order someone to do a task, but you cannot order someone to do their best or be their best. It simply does not work and usually has the opposite effect. You can influence people to do their best by providing a strong, motivating example, in addition to positive reinforcement.

Leadership addresses tasks, while influence addresses attitudes and awareness. Influence is inextricably tied to leadership.

My previous book, *Get Over It? I'm Still Going Through It*, offered a combination of my life experiences and tools for your own life. This book is not meant to show you how I lead, it is mean to help you focus on your own leadership ability and potential. As such, included are perspectives of leadership from various subject matter experts. As a leader, you must own your ability and power; no one can give it to you.

I think of people who are not in leadership positions yet are exceptional leaders from within. Your position, title, role, or project does not define you as a leader. You can lead from within. You may be a leader in the community by being a good neighbor. Or, lead at home as a parent or older sibling. Regardless of where you lead or your aspirations for leadership, there are some foundational blocks you need as you build your leadership persona.

As you read this book, I hope you will see your strength and potential. More importantly, I hope you do some necessary self-assessment. Being a leader requires constant work. Leaders are not complacent nor stagnant – well not good leaders. We have to constantly grow and develop professionally.

There are two books (found in one book) that I read years ago that taught me the most about leadership. Strangely enough it was I Kings and II Kings in the Bible. [No, I am not going to get all religious on you – though I could.] When I read them, I read them not for the spiritual motivation or to seek some kind of emotional charge. [Though that was available.] I read those books because they chronicle leaders, their strengths and failures, responses of the followers, outcomes of their decisions, and how their decisions and leadership styles impacted the leadership context of those who lead after them.

There is nothing like advice from people who have walked the path you now trod. Included in this book are life-changing words advice, caution, and encouragement from successful leaders and leadership experts. They were asked to provide advice to new and emerging leaders. Much like mentoring, the goal of the leader is to create future leaders who can carry on the legacy of an institution, region, community, country, or even family. Leadership is about serving and creating leaders. There is no room for self-doubt, ego, paralyzing fear, disrespect, bias, or divisiveness.

If you want to be a leader, you must also be a good follower. Learn to glean from other leaders and seek counsel. I am grateful to all of those who took the time to show me the rewards and perils of leadership.

Do not repeat the tactics, which have gained you one victory, but let your methods be regulated by the infinite variety of circumstances.

Sun Tzu

Chapter One:
The Evolution of Leadership

As long as there have been leaders, there have been those who tried to determine how and why they were successful. Leadership itself has not evolved, but our understanding of it has. It is important to understand why very different leadership styles can be effective, why the same leadership techniques will not work in every situation, and which leadership style fits your personality best. Everyone has leadership potential within them, but understanding these concepts will help you maximize your leadership ability.

Defining Leadership

Simply speaking, "leadership" is defined as "the ability to lead." Unfortunately, this is not very helpful. A better definition comes from the BNET online Business Dictionary: *"The capacity to establish direction and to influence and align others toward a common goal, motivating and committing them to action and making them responsible for their performance."* Although the previous statement is more descriptive, it does not tell us what leadership actually *is*, but rather what it *does*.

Characteristics of a Leader

The mark of a true leader is not a position or title held, but it is how many people are willing to follow them. Santa Clara University and the Tom Peters group outline the following leadership characteristics:

- Broad-minded

- Competent
- Courageous
- Fair-minded
- Forward-looking
- Honest
- Imaginative
- Inspiring
- Intelligent
- Straightforward

LEADERSHIP PRINCIPLES

The United States Army offers 11 Leadership Principles:

- Be tactically and technically proficient
- Develop a sense of responsibility in your subordinates
- Employ your unit in accordance with its capabilities
- Ensure the task is understood, supervised, and accomplished
- Keep your soldiers informed
- Know your soldiers and look out for their welfare
- Know yourself and seek self-improvement
- Make sound and timely decisions
- Seek responsibility and take responsibility for your actions
- Set the example
- Train your soldiers as a team

You will notice that none of the above gives guidance on *how to lead* practically and effectively. They do not address what to do or say in any given situation. That is because there is no real formula for being a leader. Leadership must come from within, and it is based on your personality. In this book, you will learn how to develop your innate leadership abilities and build the confidence required in being a true leader.

A Brief History of Leadership

HISTORICAL LEADERS

Throughout the centuries, there have been leaders. We are social animals who bond together, but we look for order to balance the chaos of life. We look to be organized to accomplish tasks as a society that we cannot perform individually. As a result, someone inevitably ends up in charge – even if that someone is a tyrant.

Leaders in the past have generally belonged to one of three categories: Political, Military, or Religious.

- Military: Sun Tzu was a military general in China from 500 B.C. He wrote the Art of War, and although he was a great military leader, his book is actually about how to *not* use armies except as a last resort, focusing more on wise political policies and strategies to prevent war.

- Political: Around 1790 B.C., Babylonian ruler Hammurabi created the codified laws, which unified his empire in what was seen as a fair order as all people were subject to the same rules.

- Religious: It may be said that religious leaders have had the greatest impact on their societies, with results that last for centuries.

Academics and political theorists use Adolf Hitler as the standard for leadership gone array. In this instance, they may not be far off. Hitler used propaganda (oral and written), manipulations of political beliefs, symbols of divisiveness and separatism, and invoked a feeling of superiority amongst his constituents all while using political schemes and strong-arming to intimidate anyone who opposes him (Burns, 1978). This tyrannical (or autocratic) leadership style is coated with enough social graces that people are excited to be a part of a collective. They create the ideal follower rather than being chosen by or set up by their potential followers. One does not need to be a political figure in order to use these tactics. Look in boardrooms, C-suites, university presidents and vice-presidents, churches, pretty much anywhere in society and you can find an example of the tyrannical leadership style. It is neither rare or common.

A leader who is lost in ambition can destroy a people, political structure, corporation, agency, or country for the sake of personal advancement and power deriving from deceptive (even self-deception) and coercive practices. Ambition should be a positive, motivating force in the pursuit of leadership success – not the reason for being a leader. Burns (1978) also posits that esteem (of self and others) issues can impact one's leadership abilities. History provides evidence of Hitler's feelings of inadequacy and public disappointments. Even a desire to change history (positively) can denote a need for self-gratification and the gratification of others – rather than facilitating change for change sake. Alexander Hamilton said that the love of fame is the "the ruling passion of the noblest minds."

Though Burns (1978, p. 3) asserts that "leader and tyrant are polar opposites," there is Kellerman (2012) who goes into great detail about the tyrannical leader. This leads one to assume that the attributes associated with leadership and tyranny are not mutually exclusive. Regardless of leadership style, a true leader inspires a shared social identity amongst his followers (Tee et al., 2013). His leadership invokes shared emotion and a collective attraction to him as a leader. There must be a transactional relationship between the leader and the follower denoting a synergy of ideas.

Bennis (2009) points out two distinct hiring practices of leaders. Leaders either hire "clones" or they hire "compensators" (Bennis, 2009). The leader that hires clones looks to his followers to mirror his desires, goals, and ideas. Such a leader is not looking for critical feedback or substantive discourse. Rather than hiring compensators, a tyrannical leader will hire "yes-men" or "yes-women" to help them achieve the vision in the manner that they envision it (ensuring personal goals as well as collective goals are met).

Modern Leaders

With the rise of the industrial revolution, a new kind of leader emerged: Economic. The so-called Captains of Industry found they could build an empire based on modern technology instead of swords. Oil Barons, railroad magnates, and factory owners built large fortunes without the benefit of armies; it was often at the expense of the people they employed. This gave rise to Union leaders and various movements designed to promote justice where abuses were perceived to exist.

The Industrial Revolution also increased the number of Scientific Leaders, as scientists now had easy access to a wide range of new materials for their work. Psychiatry and Psychology came into prominence with studies on the workplace, in regards to improving productivity and the effect on the workforce.

Studies show that workers are more productive when they are in a "positive work environment." The attitude and influence of the boss is a major factor in this productivity. If employees feel they are listened to, respected, and treated fairly, they are happier in their work and perform better than those who feel they are disrespected and unappreciated. Which kind of work environment would *you* prefer?

Three Theories of Leadership

THE GREAT MAN THEORY

The Great Man Theory was abandoned in favor of the theories of behavioral science. It's easy to be inspired by stories of great men and women who did great things in their lives. Alexander the Great conquered the known world. Genghis Khan then ravaged most of it. Abraham Lincoln freed the slaves. Harriet Tubman saved hundreds from slavery in the Underground Railroad. Mother Theresa aided and comforted thousands in Calcutta who were abandoned by society. The theory goes that these people did great things because they were simply great people determined by fate and fulfilling their destiny.

The Trait Theory

It has often been said, *"Great leaders are born, not made."* Trait Theory takes this saying literally - lead, you were born with it, with no way of learning those skills. This theory expands on the Great Man Theory by defining what makes great leaders "great."

Today, we recognize that true leadership seems to come from a combination of both theories – and more. As we have seen, there are wide varieties of leadership qualities. Everyone has some ability in at least one or more of these areas. This means that under the right circumstances, anyone can rise to a leadership role and be successful based on the leadership style that best matches his or her personality – if the person knows how to use that ability to address the situation at hand properly. Other leadership skills can indeed be learned, developed, and mastered.

Transformational Leadership

In 1978, James MacGregor Burns introduced the idea of transformational leadership as he researched political leaders. Burns theorized that "transformational leadership" is a process where leaders interact with their followers and inspire each other to advance together. His characteristics and behaviors demonstrated the differences between "management" and "leadership." Transformation within a person or an organization is as effective as the leadership style and abilities of the leader. A true leader can convey the vision and mission while guiding the transformation.

Bernard M. Bass, in 1985, added to Burns' transformational leadership theory by shifting the focus to the followers. It is not the individual traits and vision of the leader that matter as much as they can influence the feelings, attitudes, and commitment of their followers. As we mentioned before in productivity studies, if followers feel they can trust a leader (or better yet, if they admire a leader who can stimulate a sense of loyalty and respect) the followers go beyond what was originally expected of them and will do so happily. As a result, productivity and unity increases. A charismatic, motivational leader transforms the followers.

Leadership requires creativity. A leader must be flexible and open to innovative discovery. The inspirational or transformational leader will encourage creativity in their followers. More important than fostering creativity, a leadership style must not inhibit creativity. The right leadership in the wrong context reveals that the organization has the wrong leader. Creativity is not a by-product of leadership; it is essential to leadership. The growth and effectiveness of an organization are dependent upon innovation (group creativity). There must be an atmosphere conducive to the generation and production of ideas. Followers must feel safe to present and challenge ideas. Leaders must be willing to collaborate.

Summary

Through all of the studies, we have seen that there are a variety of attributes and abilities associated with leadership, and these vary from leader to leader. Some leaders are great orators, others great writers. Some leaders are very quiet, but the force of their logic or passion wins the day. The difference between a good leader and a great leader is partly the number of leadership skills they have developed. The other part is their ability to apply those skills properly to those who would follow. We will address these issues in the next section.

Practical Illustration

Julie and Mindy had worked side by side for over five years. They chatted between projects and took lunch breaks together. When the company restructured, Julie was given a management position, and Mindy became her subordinate. Mindy felt that it was unfair that she now had to take instructions from Julie and her negative attitude caused the department to lose productivity. Julie understood that it would take time to earn back Mindy's respect. She kept a positive attitude when working with Mindy and always kept Mindy informed of things that were relevant to Mindy's job. She assigned tasks to Mindy that she knew Mindy could accomplish and she gave appropriate feedback when work was delivered. Julie took responsibility for her decisions and did not blame others when things went wrong. Over time, she gained Mindy's respect, and the department's productivity soared.

You manage things; you lead people.

Murray Hopper

Advice for a U.S. Army Veteran: Kurt Schoenig

Kurt Schoenig

Email: kschoenig@vanguardfine.com

Company: Vanguard-Fine, LLC

Mr. Kurt Schoenig is a commercial real estate agent of a few months. Though, he proudly served in the U.S. Army as an Infantryman for 8 years. He was deployed to Iraq and Afghanistan. Mr. Schoenig says, "The military brings with it some of the most professional people I've met and also the most unprofessional as well." He continued, "Sadly, the poor performers get picked up for leadership positions at all levels. The juxtaposition is easy to spot, and you can't just give your two weeks notice when you have a bad leader."

Don't Get Comfortable

"One of the biggest deficiencies I see in "bad" leaders is complacency. If the leader has been at one specific position for an extended period of time, they begin to go unchecked. They can hide behind the position of authority and begin to stagnate their own progress most times unknowingly. It's human nature to seek out the easiest way of doing things, that goes for being a leader and personal growth. Recognizing that and taking measures to push yourself out of your comfort zone in anything can help one remember back to [the] feeling of doing something new for the first time. This can also check one's ego as to remind one they don't know how to do everything at the level they do at work."

*Mr. Schoenig, Sir, thank you for your service and your continued dedication to excellence in leadership.

Chapter Two:
Context and Narrative

What is context? The answer can become complicated. Put simply, context is the nature, culture, personality, composition, history, and overall shared experience of the organization. When becoming a leader, the question is not whether the project, department, or organization is a "good-fit" for you. The true question: *Is this what is best for me and the organization, both individually and collectively?*

Leadership requires a balance between one's ambitions, the need of one's followers, desires and directives of the leader's leaders, and the overarching goal (or best interest) of the institution or organization. Secondarily, in the pursuit of successful outcomes, a leader understands the importance and value of strategic relationships. It is essential that a leader realizes that leadership is about forging, managing, and growing relationships, and separate from the business of mergers, acquisitions, and takeovers (hostile in instances). An effective leader is one who can recognize and lead within the institutional context (Bennis, 2009; Liden & Antonakis, 2009). Context comprises all within the virtual and tangible physical and social spaces of an institution (Liden & Antonakis, 2009). It may be difficult, but a leader must set aside personal ambition for successes and fame when it distracts or competes with the shared vision of the organization or when the pursuit of personal achievements weakens the morale of one's followers.

Often, I find that the dilemma that emerging leaders face is not whether they are a good leader, but whether he or she is pursuing leadership within the proper arena. You may be a great leader within a high-stakes corporate context, but only mediocre in a non-profit organization. According to Burns (1978), powerful influences derive from the exchange of ideas (engagement) between two or more individuals or groups; thus, the transactional nature of leadership-followership.

The grand narrative of an organization encompasses internal and external organizational challenges
(Faris & Parry, 2011).

Ronald Reagan before and during his presidency was very aware of context and the pulse of the American people. Reagan, as noted by Bennis (2009), was considered the "Teflon President." Reagan, "proved leadership is a performance art" (Bennis, 2009, p. 38). The art of leadership exists not in one's ability to perform but one's ability to perform given a specific context and group of followers. President Reagan saw the fears and mistrust of the American people – Russia, Iran, and the U.S. government itself. By understanding the context, Reagan sought to bring cohesiveness to the country. Reagan understood that the only way to simultaneously achieve his goals and the goals of his Party was to acknowledge and address the fears of the people. Bennis (2009) said that Reagan did this by projecting authenticity, genuineness, and seemingly without pretense. I am not a fan of the Reagan agenda or political decisions, but I feel it is important to mention his handle on leadership given the context of that time. His authentic leadership impacts the Republican Party even today.

Besides context, some leaders struggle with communication style and effectiveness. Franklin D. Roosevelt (FDR) and Abraham Lincoln were both very measured, consistent, direct, and calm in tone and demeanor – the same is said for Barak Obama. Bennis (2009) says that Lincoln and FDR knew how to "rise above personal disappointments and hurts" to lead the American people. A leader cannot be easily excited or unabridged in their commentaries on current events. You must be aware of the context given the grand narrative!

Leaders are artists; leadership is an art form. A great leader will be able to evoke positive, desirable, responses from his followers. A leader must understand not only how to lead but how to lead given the context and the particular group of followers. To that end, creativity is a fluid concept. It is concrete in its varying forms – visual, vocal, theoretical, tactile, authentic, flawed, simplistic, abstract, modern, revolutionary, focused, direct, indirect, light, shaded, etc. Like art, leadership appears differently depending on the atmosphere in which it is placed – light, dark, sun, artificial light, etc.

A leader must be aware of the grand narrative and must create a leadership plan that will address the idiosyncrasies associated with individual followers and groups of followers. The grand narrative includes external context (and challenges), organizational culture, individual leadership, and organizational effectiveness. The grand narrative consists of any cultural, political, sociological, psychological, religious, familial, or another factor that encompasses the external context. A leader must consider the impact of the external factors on the organization. Also included in the grand narrative are the static and dynamic elements of the organization – leadership, followership, and effectiveness.

Three Mistakes of Bad Leaders: Lleuella Morris

Lleuella Morris

Personal Growth Expert and Mentor

Creator and Managing Director of AMZ Consulting Company, Ltd

amzconsultco@gmail.com

Phone: 18687331044

Lleuella Morris writes and conducts workshops on personal growth and works with people to grow themselves. An avid volunteer, she served on the Board of the Association of Female Executives of Trinidad and Tobago; volunteered with the United Nations online and sat on the Advisory Committee of the Children's Ministry Department of the South Caribbean Conference of Seventh-day Adventists in Trinidad.

According to her blog: Lleuella successfully grew herself through adverse life situations and now helps liberate people and set them free by sharing knowledge and creating tools, techniques, systems, and frameworks to grow and develop them. She gifts people with the gift of self-knowledge and self-awareness and context to solve their difficult life situations.

"THE GROWTH AND DEVELOPMENT OF PEOPLE IS THE HIGHEST CALLING OF LEADERSHIP". ~HARVEY FIRESTONE

Sometimes you need to know if you are doing it wrong or in danger of doing it wrong. I turned to Ms. Morris for her thought on a bad leader. She said, "From my experience serving under and alongside all kinds of leaders, I believe bad leaders can become excellent leaders if they do three things.

1. See themselves as the organizational developers

Perhaps the first mistake is that new leaders fail to see themselves as Organizational Developers. With the 'changing of the guards' there is a renewing of expectations of new and better possibilities, and change. By virtue of this, a leader is tasked with initiating and managing organizational change. While many new leaders understand this in theory, instead of initiating a collaborative process through formal knowledge gathering, they quickly settle in to a command and control approach, falsely believing that this will get them to their destination faster. What results instead is that the leader becomes a one-man show, fails to secure employee trust and buy-in, and fails to achieve even their well-intentioned plans.

This approach does not work simply because it violates the basic principle that the more contribution employees make toward a thing, the more committed they are likely to be to it. If employees were not initially engaged, then we can be sure they have no vested emotional interest in your plans.

2. Should not presume they know what the situation is and how they will fix it

The second mistake is that persons who have come through the ranks and are transitioning to new leadership position often feel that they know exactly what the organization's challenges are and how they will fix it. Even in cases of external transitions, because the incoming may have a source or have been briefed either formally or informally, they falsely hold that they are knowledgeable enough to transform the entity to the success they believe it should achieve. This cannot be determined in the absence of engaging employees in an initial assessment or feedback.

What results is that the plans put forward are often relevant only to the leader and a few employees, and there is a dwindling of employee support when the novelty of new leadership has worn off. There is no true buy-in and the leader fails.

As a new leader you must not presume that you know the situation for the following reasons:

- ✓ Your source may have conducted the primary research and therefore that was his/ her reality. However, once told to you, it becomes secondary information to you and you must initiate a process to secure your primary data in order to determine your reality.

- ✓ Not because the information was true for your source(s), means it will be true for you.

- ✓ Regardless of how well-informed or well-intentioned your source(s), objectivity must be the order of your day.

- ✓ Regardless of how thorough your source(s), they may have missed critical pieces of data.

- ✓ Regardless of what obtained in the past, what obtains presently is the current and correct thing and therefore all you need be concerned with. Your source(s) information is not up to date.

- ✓ Regardless of how knowledgeable your source(s), they hold conscious or sub-conscious bias.

3. Believe that seeking initial feedback from their constituents make them look weak or incompetent

. The human tendency toward independence and self-sufficiency in order to maintain respect of those they manage is an error in judgement that ultimately results in the very thing it was intended to safe guard against. Simply because, a leader cannot properly manage a thing he or she doesn't have adequate knowledge of. This results in certain failure.

Chapter Three:
Situational Leadership

Now we get to the real core of leadership. The definitive leadership style research comes from Paul Hersey and Kenneth Blanchard, which they expressed in their Situational Leadership Model. The Hersey-Blanchard model addresses the key to practical leadership development: the attributes and styles of the *followers*.

Not everyone is on the same intellectual, maturity, compliance, or motivational level. Different people are motivated by different things, and this must be considered if one is to be a great leader. Communications experts consider it critical to tailor your message to your "target audience." It is the followers that you want to motivate and influence and you cannot do that if you do not know whom you are trying to motivate or influence.

The Situational Leadership model addresses four types of leadership styles, based on the follower:

- Participating

- Selling

- Delegating

- Telling

The goal is to develop followers to the Delegating level as seen in the figure:

Leadership Styles in the Hersey-Blanchard Situational Leadership Model

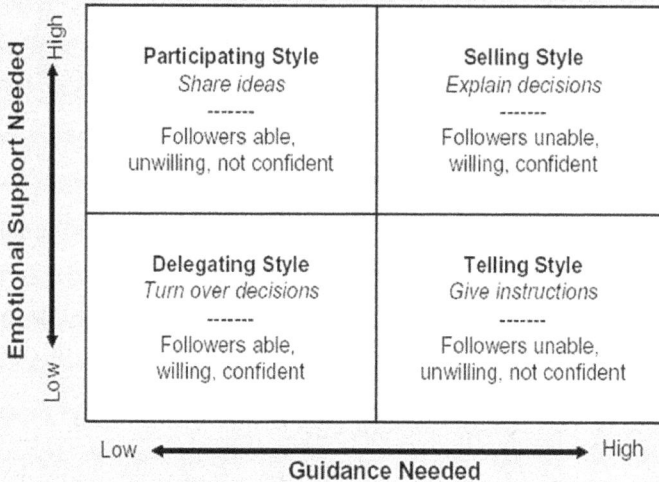

	Low ← Guidance Needed → **High**
High Emotional Support Needed **Low**	

Participating Style *Share ideas* ------- Followers able, unwilling, not confident	**Selling Style** *Explain decisions* ------- Followers unable, willing, confident
Delegating Style *Turn over decisions* ------- Followers able, willing, confident	**Telling Style** *Give instructions* ------- Followers unable, unwilling, not confident

Low ◄─────────► **High**
Guidance Needed

Situational Leadership: Telling

Telling is the lowest level of leadership style. Most new employees require direct instructions, so this is called the "Telling" or "Directing" style. The follower is characterized by low competence and high commitment, being unable to comply, with possible feelings of insecurity.

The leader must focus highly on tasks, rather than a relationship with the employee, as a relationship does not yet exist.

When an employee cannot do the job because they are unknowledgeable, the leader must spend much more time working with the employee, offering clear instructions and regular follow up. The leader must be encouraging and motivational, offering praise for positive results and correction for less than positive results. The idea is to motivate the follower to rise to the next level of ability.

This is a very leader-driven stage.

Situational Leadership: Selling

Selling addresses the follower who has developed some competence with an improved commitment. The follower is not convinced yet, but is open to becoming cooperative and motivated.

The leader must still focus highly on tasks and this still requires much of the leader's time, but the focus now also includes developing a relationship with the employee. Build upon the trust that has begun to develop and the encouragement that has been demonstrated. The leader must spend more time listening and offering advice, scheduling the follower for additional training if the situation requires it.

The goal is to engage the follower so they can develop to the next level. There is less "telling" and more "suggesting" which leads to more encouragement and acting as a coach. It is recognition that they have progressed and this motivates them to progress even further.

This is a very leader-driven stage.

Situational Leadership: Participating

Participating addresses the follower who is now competent at the job, but remains somewhat inconsistent and is not yet fully committed. The follower may be uncooperative or performing as little work as possible, despite their competence with the tasks.

The leader must participate with and support the follower. The leader no longer needs to give detailed instructions and follow up as often, but does need to continue working with the follower to ensure the work is being done at the level required.

The follower is now highly competent, but is not yet convinced in his or her ability or not fully committed to do their best and excel. The leader must now focus less on the tasks assigned and more on the relationship between the follower, the leader, and the group.

This is a very follower-driven, relationship-focused stage.

Situational Leadership: Delegating

Delegating is the ultimate goal: a follower who feels fully empowered and competent enough to take the ball and run with it, with minimal supervision. The follower is highly competent, highly committed, motivated, and empowered.

The leader can now delegate tasks to the follower and observe with minimal follow up, knowing that acceptable or even excellent results will be achieved. There is a low focus on tasks and a low focus on relationships. There is no need to compliment the follower on every task, although continued praise for outstanding performance must be given as appropriate.

This is a very follower-driven stage.

Practical Illustration

Jackie became frustrated with her staff members. She said to her manager, "I feel like I'm putting in 120%. I'm exhausted!"

Paulette frowned a little. "Whenever I hear that, I feel like perhaps the leader is working so hard because they are doing things that might be the jobs of the followers."

Jackie admitted, "I give a lot of detailed information and follow up with my employees very frequently, just to make sure everything goes perfectly."

Paulette was honest with her. "While it's great that you're so attentive, perhaps your staff is feeling micromanaged. Even if you're afraid that something might go awry, if you step back to let them to carry out tasks on their own, you may ultimately see better results."

Jackie took Paulette's advice. When she trusted her employees, things went much more smoothly.

Courage - not complacency - is our need today.

Leadership not salesmanship.

John F. Kennedy

Chapter Four:
A Personal Inventory

In 2002, Jossey Bass published a book by James Kouzes, and Barry Posner called *The Leadership Challenge*. Building upon the Hersey-Blanchard model and other transformational leadership models, they went to the heart of what skills are required by the leader to stimulate such a transformation. What abilities can influence followers and bring them to accept the leader's vision as their own?

An Introduction to Kouzes and Posner

James Kouzes and Barry Posner asked thousands of people to rank a list of characteristics associated with leadership, including the seven top qualities that motivated them to follow willingly. They gave this survey to over 75,000 people over a 20-year period.

In their book, *The Leadership Challenge* the authors identified five abilities that were crucial to successful leadership:

- **Model the Way**: You must lead by example. You cannot come into work 10 minutes late every day if you want your employees to arrive on time.

- **Inspire a Shared Vision**: If you capture the imagination, you will inspire creative thought and increase loyalty. The vision does not need to be grandiose, but it needs to be communicated effectively for others to adopt it as one of their own.

- **Challenge the Process**: Do not continue doing something just because "We've always done it that way." Situations change, and sometimes a policy or procedure never worked well in the first place. Think outside the box.

- **Enable Others to Act**: Truly empower people to act on their own at their level of authority. The famed Ritz-Carlton hotel empowers every employee at all levels to spend up to $1000 on behalf of a guest (who is informed reimbursement is required for whatever request they make).

- **Encourage the Heart**: A positive attitude is infectious. If the leader appears passionate or excited about the vision, others will catch the enthusiasm as well.

A PERSONAL INVENTORY

The results of the Kouzes and Posner study, with the most important quality at the top:

• Broad-minded	• Ambitious
• Competent	• Caring
• Dependable	• Cooperative
• Fair-minded	• Courageous
• Forward-looking	• Determined
• Honest	• Imaginative
• Inspiring	• Independent
• Intelligent	• Loyal
• Straightforward	• Mature
• Supportive	• Self-controlled

Creating an Action Plan

Now that you understand the various concepts, it's time to plan how to put them into action by incorporating them into your life.

Set Leadership Goals: In leadership, as in life, you will never come to the end of your learning, but you want to rank in priority order those qualities you want to develop.

Address the Goals: Determine how you will accomplish your goals. Do you feel you need to learn more about teamwork so you can better lead a team? Join a team sport. Do you want to communicate better? Take a creative writing class or join Toastmasters and get some public speaking experience. Toastmasters are also great if you are shy and want to feel more comfortable in social situations.

Seek Inspiration: Learn about a variety of leaders, including their styles in dealing with challenges. Read books and conduct research on the internet or at libraries.

Choose a Role Model: Based on your research, choose a role model that fits your personality. You might choose a dynamic leader like Teddy Roosevelt or an intellectual leader like Albert Schweitzer or Albert Einstein. Read several biographies and find videos on his or her life.

Seek Experience: Take a leadership role in a social group or club. Gain experience working with people on many levels.

Create a Personal Mission Statement: Imagine your legacy. How do you want to be remembered? What do you want people to think of you? What type of leader did you decide to be? Write a statement that defines who you will become.

Practical Illustration

Yolanda was not sure why the morale of her employees was down. She'd modeled the way. She had communicated their shared vision. Yolanda had made changes and fostered a workplace which rewarded ingenuity. She worked on enabling others to act, to have her employees exert their authority. It was only when she went back to her training manual on Leadership that she realized what she'd been missing.

Yolanda entered the meeting room with a new, more positive attitude. She started by showing enthusiasm and passion for their tasks at hand. She made sure to smile during the meeting. Of course, she had to be an authority figure, when it was realistic, she found ways to genuinely compliment others to show them that their work was appreciated. It was clear that the manual was right. 'A positive attitude is infectious.'

Some look at things that are, and ask why. I dream of things that never were and ask why not?

George Bernard Shaw

Self-Management and Core Competencies: Dr. Alexander Lowry

Alexander Lowry

Professor of Finance at Gordon College

Director for the Master of Science in Financial Analysis

www.linkedin.com/in/alexanderlowry

Alexander Lowry, Professor of Finance at Gordon College and also the Director for the Master of Science in Financial Analysis program. He was previously a Chief Operating Officer at J.P. Morgan in New York City. Find Professor Lowry on LinkedIn at www.linkedin.com/in/alexanderlowry or on Twitter at https://twitter.com/AlexanderSLowry. Find out more about the Gordon College Finance Program at http://www.gordon.edu/graduate/finance.

Here is what Prof. Lowry had to say:

"I'm a professor of finance at Gordon College and director of the school's Master of Science in Financial Analysis program. In addition, I'm an Advisor and Board of Directors Member for fintech and financial services companies. Which means I'm transforming, accelerating, and advising businesses that students I'm educating want to work for.

As a professor, I help students understand how the financial services industry works. I also lead a master's in financial analysis program, helping students bridge their liberal arts background to a focused career in finance.

As a Board member, I work with fintech and financial services companies that want to transform traditional industry business models to unleash exponential growth and value. I bring expertise in governance, strategy. growth, financial management and operations.

As a CEO advisor, I mentor CEOs and Boards who want to turn strategy into action. Currently working with 20+ early stage and middle market businesses.

Good leadership:

A good leader is strong in five core competencies: self-management, organizational capabilities, team building and teamwork, problem solving, and sustaining the vision. The competencies represent a hierarchy, so each competency builds on the ones before it. Self-management is at the bottom: You can't excel in any domain until you're able to regulate your own thoughts, emotions, and habits. This is according to the CPI 260, a personality test designed to assess leadership potential. The output from taking the test, which includes someone's ratings in 18 key areas such as decisiveness and the ability to handle sensitive problems, is based on years of research on the factors that go into effective management. The CPI 260 and the reports that come with the results are used by major companies including Red Cross, AIM Investment Services, and Delta Associates."

Chapter Five:
Inspiring a Shared Vision

The key to true leadership is to inspire a shared vision among your followers. Before you can convey a vision, however, you must develop it. You must be clear in your vision, live it before others can see it, and model it from your behavior. Bennis (2009) explains that strategic planning requires strategic thinking that requires direction, a destination, a mission, and vision. As a leader, you may need to recapture and communicate a revised mission and vision for the organization. Doing so may require that you work within the context to identify individuals that can help shape the shared vision. Why not create a shared vision rather than get your followers to share in your vision? Okay, so that is not always possible or expedient – but consider it.

Authenticity

An emerging leader must be able to comfortably answer the following questions: (1) About what are you passionate? (2) What can you do that will ignite passion with you (individually and organization-wide)? (3) Do you feel you are doing what you are best at doing? (4) Is there anything that you are doing that you are (a) not best at or (b) not passionate about? These questions will help you better ascertain your potential quality and effectiveness as a leader. Self-awareness, as discussed in the chapter on Personal Inventory, is important for authenticity. People will not embrace your vision; they will embrace a *shared vision*.

In order to employ Authentic Leadership, leaders first know themselves – truly and without a filter. This self-awareness will empower the leaders to be comfortable in their leadership positions. Authenticity is contagious. It means that you, as a leader, must be open and willing to reveal your true self to your followers. Yagil and Medler-Liraz (2014) stated, "Authentic leadership thus comprises several interrelated dimensions: self-awareness, balanced processing, authentic behavior, and authentic relational orientation." So, while the concepts have differences, the necessity of self-awareness (in varying forms) is undeniable. An authentic leader must be cautious not to be too transparent. Authenticity is being real in a way that does not cause self-sabotage.

When a leader is comfortable with who they are as a person (past and present), who they are as a leader, and their ability to handle the power inherent in their role, their followers will be more trusting and freer to themselves be authentic. Authenticity is innovative. An authentic leader is gutsy and willing to take steps that others are unwilling to take (Bennis, 2009). We must also know that innovation is a by-product of collaboration. Change the leaders, and the followers will change. Bring out the passion in the leaders, and you will begin to see passionate followers.

Leader-followership requires a connection – attachment. I saw attachment theory at its finest when I was working with trustees and board of directors at vastly different organizations. It always amazes me how often I am in a meeting where there are seemingly mature and accomplished people who revert to childhood hurt or comfort. Because authentic leaders "foster authenticity" in their followers, there is a nurturing that takes place. A follower with unhealthy or weak ("insecure") attachments may be avoidant and not receptive to this leadership style. Take time to observe interactions and non-verbal responses to see whether an individual follower is accepting, avoidant, or ambivalent.

Authenticity is not synonymous with ethicality; neither is it an achievable leadership goal (Algera & Lips-Wiersma, 2012). Reagan, FDR, and Obama were proponents of transparency and authenticity in government as well as leadership. All learned rather quickly that true authenticity opened them up to excessive criticisms and unwanted advice and proceeded with a 'radical authentic leadership' (Algera & Lips-Wiersma, 2012). The success of a leader, political or otherwise, rests firmly in an individual's ability to identify, personalize, empathize, and respond to the context of the time, given the grand narrative, all while being selectively transparent and truly authentic.

Choosing Your Vision

What do you want to accomplish, and what do you need to do to get there? Determine attainable goals and focus on them. King Arthur sought the Holy Grail. Lewis and Clark mapped much of the United States. NASA took us to the moon. What is your vision?

Your vision will provide a sense of direction for you and your followers. In the military, the focus is on "the mission." Whatever the mission is, everyone is dedicated to it. Let your vision be like a lighthouse on a hill, guiding ships to safety and warning them away from the rocks.

Communicating Your Vision

Communication is more than just the words you say or the memos you write. Remember, actions speak louder than words. Take every opportunity to communicate your vision in words and deeds. One of the best ways to communicate a vision is to sum it up in a simple catchphrase.

Post your slogan, catchphrase and mission statement in prominent locations. When you send out emails, list it in quotes below your signature block. Hold meetings occasionally or hand out "Visionary Awards" to people who exemplify your vision. Above all, lead by example.

I worked with one organization that required recitation of the mission and vision statements at each meeting or placed on the way of all meeting rooms. The organization embodied the vision; it became a part of every decision. There is nothing like saying, "How does this tie into the mission and vision of the organization?" That simple question communicates to staff that regardless of how excellent the proposal, no proposal is accepted unless it is consistent with the collective vision and mission.

Identifying the Benefit for Others

Answer the question, "What's in it for me?" as if you were one of your own followers. The answer might not always be obvious. Certainly, performance bonuses and awards work, but most followers enjoy being part of a larger, successful organization. Everyone loves a winner. When the home team wins at the stadium, you would think the fans in the stand were the players by the way they share in the victory and excitement. Leaders are givers, not leaches. They look for what they can give to their followers, inspiring positive morale and dedicated professionals. If your followers cannot create their own satisfactory answer to the "what's in it for me" question, then they will either become a bottleneck or you will have high turnover. Benefits in this case are not the same as those benefits and perks handled by HR. Each employee has their own life goals and visions. They need to be able to answer how he work they do, your vision, and the collective vision empowers them as an individual and professionally,

We are social creatures who like to feel like we belong. We crave acceptance. If you can get your followers to accept your vision as their own, and excite them about being part of it, they will often excel beyond what you (or they) thought possible. Be sure to reward loyalty and performance above and beyond the call of duty. In that vein, remember to reward progress even if the goal is not yet reached or the performance levels are not yet where they need to be. It will make your followers want to contribute more.

Practical Illustration

Bruce spoke passionately about his company's vision. He believed in their product, and he wanted his employees to feel the same enthusiasm. He'd been wracking his brain for a way to instill this in his followers as their leader. One day, the answer came to him.

He got nice paper and printed out certificates. He also bought small prizes, like candies, brightly colored office supplies, and lottery tickets. He waited until Sean, one of his newer employees, used his own enthusiasm and passion for securing a new client.

Bruce announced to the office. "I'd just like to take a moment to congratulate Sean on his new client. He used his enthusiasm for our product to sign them on. I'd like to give him this Visionary Award for exemplifying our vision."

Bruce continued to give out these awards, inspiring his employees to become excited about their vision.

Leadership: the art of getting someone else to do something you want done because he wants to do it.

Dwight D. Eisenhower

It's About Attitude: Sophie Miles

Sophie Miles

VP of Marketing & Co-Founder

CalculatorBuddy.com

Sophie Miles, VP of Marketing & Co-Founder of Calculator-Buddy.com, a tech company in expansion to USA, Canada, and South Africa. They have almost 10 years of experience in Internet entrepreneurship in Europe. Within a few years, they fleshed out the concept, wrote a business plan and set it up. Now they are leaders in all region, selling out our products even to our competitors.

"What makes someone a successful leader? I would answer: <u>Form new leaders</u>.

Leading does not mean having blind followers in the company, but also forming new leaders of those followers. No project or idea is sustained in time without continuity. A leadership without succession is a dead end and it generates dependent and weak work teams. Even it could endanger the work itself and the continuity of the organization.

Leading is to inspire the construction of a better future, dedicating itself to the formation and transformation of people to be better human beings, parents, children, spouses, friends, and professionals. Anyway, better people, because before being a good leader you have to be a good human being.

Keep in mind this advice is directly related to attitudes and behavior. It does not require any special training or birth skill. In other words, it is not your knowledge or skills that will make a difference in your leadership, but your attitude."

Chapter Six:
Quality Leaders Produce Quality Leaders

Remember that the best leaders are examples of what they want their followers to be. George Washington rode into battle with his troops. You cannot lead from the rear sending your followers out to take the heat and face the challenges while you remain in an ivory tower – eliminating any possibility of respect.

By definition, a leader is in the *lead*, right up front, ready to take the heat if something goes wrong. If something does go wrong, a true leader never blames his followers, even if in fact they failed. A true leader takes the blame and then addresses how to correct the problems that arose. The quality of the follower is tied directly to the quality of the leader and the quality of the leadership (Bennis, 2009).

Determining Your Way

Once you have chosen your role model, study what qualities made them successful. Learn about what challenges they faced and how the challenges were met. Learn about the ideas and philosophies that drove them and made them successful. Study, again, the Hersey-Blanchard model and see how different situations called for different styles of leadership.

Since there is no leader in history who has escaped life without experiencing failures, pay particular attention to how your hero deals with adversity. George Washington nearly lost the American Revolution through major hesitations in leadership; and, in fact, he lost New York to the British general William Howe, Washington learned from his mistakes and the rest, as they say, is history.

Being an Inspirational Role Model

Leadership is neither for the timid nor for the arrogant. Often confidence is resented or misinterpreted as arrogance. People who lack self-confidence can feel intimidated by a true leader. Do not allow intimidation or your assessment of the strength and successes of others hold you back. If you have honesty, integrity, and deal with everyone fairly, then others will see that. Be willing to listen to criticism, but also consider the source. If you are too afraid of what others might say about you, or you ignore legitimate complaints insisting on respect solely because of your position, you will lose the respect and cooperation of your followers and peers.

President Theodore Roosevelt said:

"It is not the critic who counts; not the man who points out how the strong man stumbles, or where the doer of deeds could have done them better. The credit belongs to the man who is actually in the arena, whose face is marred by dust and sweat and blood, who strives valiantly; who errs and comes short again and again; because there is not effort without error and shortcomings; but who does actually strive to do the deed; who knows the great enthusiasm, the great devotion, who spends himself in a worthy cause, who at the best knows in the end the triumph of high achievement and who at the worst, if he fails, at least he fails while daring greatly. So that his place shall never be with those cold and timid souls who know neither victory nor defeat."

Influencing Others' Perspectives

You may have heard that perception is reality. You must always present an honest, caring, dedicated attitude to inspire others. To inspire loyalty, you must have a track record of honesty and fairness. If any of your followers do feel they were wronged, for whatever reason, you need to address the issue immediately. People talk, and a problem ignored is a problem that grows.

Believe it or not, the most powerful influence you can have is often not trying to influence someone. When people believe you are open to their suggestions and believe they have been heard, they will work harder even if they disagree with the methods or goals. That is the power of listening. Simply listening to others makes them feel empowered, even if you do not accept their suggestions. If a follower feels there's no point talking to you, they will not, and they will disengage themselves from your vision and will only follow your directions begrudgingly.

If your followers see you as going the extra mile, they are more likely to go the extra mile, as well. If you hide in your office and people never see you, you will be perceived as out of the loop, uninformed, uninterested, and therefore, unworthy to lead. Many a successful corporate executive makes it a point to be seen by their employees every day. If an employee is to be commended for something, do so publicly, right in the middle of the workplace while their coworkers surround them. That sends a powerful message to everyone.

Practical Illustration

Justin has had a difficult time being a leader lately. Things have just felt monotonous and stale, and he was wondering why he'd ever wanted to be a leader in the first place. He sat down to talk with the leader of another group of employees to refocus.

Amy listened to Justin, and then she asked him, "In the past when you dreamed about becoming a leader, what other leaders inspired you?"

Justin thought about this for a moment, and then he said, "I've always been inspired by Martin Luther King, Jr. He was powerful and peaceful at the same time. He was courageous, and he stood up for his beliefs."

Amy smiled. "How can you use his example to inspire and influence your followers?"

This got Justin thinking, and before he knew it, he had a list of ideas for how he could reinvigorate his staff and himself.

I suppose leadership at one time meant muscles; but today it means getting along with people.

Mohandas K. Gandhi

Commitment to Developing and Empowering: Joanna Tropp-Bluestone

Joanna Tropp-Bluestone

Career & Life Strategist and founder of Negotiation Geek www.negotiationgeek.com

Joanna Tropp-Bluestone has more than 15 years of experience in corporate leadership development, talent management, organizational development and consulting. She has a B.A. from University of Michigan and an M.A.in Organizational Psychology from Columbia University. Joanna coaches leaders at all levels helping them to navigate their biggest challenges and achieve their loftiest career goals. In her spare time, Ms. Tropp-Bluestone, Joanna, enjoys cooking, traveling, scuba diving and playing Scrabble.

Joanna offers a well-balanced take on the personality of true leaders. Here is her perspective:

"Leadership is anointed, not appointed," one of my clients replied when asked about his leadership philosophy. After years of coaching stressed-out, underperforming leaders, those words resonated with me. It can be eye-opening when leaders realize that their titles don't guarantee credibility or respect, but instead, must be earned.

While a myriad of traits make leaders successful, one of the most underrated is a commitment to developing and empowering their direct reports.

Leaders should be keenly aware of their direct reports' strengths, development needs and career aspirations.

These should be discussed periodically throughout the year. Effective leaders make sure that their team members know what is expected of them, feel comfortable voicing concerns and asking for help when necessary, and are assigned projects which help them grow.

New and seasoned managers often find delegation challenging, especially when initiatives are highly visible or the stakes are high. However, by trying to do everything themselves, these managers

*overextend themselves, risk fatigue, illness and reduced perfor-
mance stemming from being overworked and lacking sufficient
time to get everything done. In addition, they are depriving employees of opportunities to take on new challenges, learn more
about the business and master new skills.*

*There are many leaders who delegate tasks to their direct reports
without proper guidance or direction or fail to check that the employee understands what is expected. When the completed project
falls short of expectations, it can be tempting for the leader to fix it
him/herself, but this deprives the direct report of a valuable development opportunity. When faced with situations like these, effective leaders talk with their direct report to understand whether
there was a breakdown in communication, why he/she chose a
certain approach, how the final product falls short of expectations
and how it can be fixed. Clearly, this approach takes more time
than the leader simply fixing the work him/herself but helps the
employee learn and grow. It also provides the leader with valuable
feedback - he/she might not have outlined expectations clearly
enough or might have overestimated their employee's knowledge
or skill.*

*Effective leaders provide feedback regularly and make sure that
employees know where they stand. Giving an employee corrective
feedback is never fun, but good leaders take the time to have these
conversations when they observe the behavior (rather than wait-
ing until performance review time). Feedback should be seen as a
gift - when someone invests time and energy to tell you how you're
perceived by others or what you can do to improve, they are helping you better yourself.*

*Good leaders often find it helpful to have standing, one-on-one
meetings with their direct reports weekly. This is a great opportunity to share feedback, review progress the employee is making
toward his/her goals and what assistance or resources he/she
needs"*

So, You Know You are a Bad Leader: Wayne Strickland

Mr. Wayne Strickland, successful 25-year Vice Presi-dent at Hall-mark Cards, has extraordinary experienc-es to share that include winning and losing billion-dollar contracts. His success and failures have informed his approach to building a competitive culture with enlightened leadership. He's a former Senior Executive at Hall-mark with 38 years in Cus-tomer-Facing, Strategy Development, Marketing, and Product Development roles. In his 35th year in the business, he led the launch and development of the Hallmark Greet-ings business across multiple Amazon platforms. His strategic thinking, team building, and enlightened leadership will drive any business. His ex-perience includes team leader for all Mass Channel customers in North America, including Walmart, Sam's, Target, Su-permarket and Drug Channels. Mr. Strickland's day-to-day leader-ship responsibilities in-clude execution in 20k rooftops and man-agement of 15k employees. To add, he is a published author on sub-jects including leadership, communication, and decision-making skills. I recommend you read his book, *Get Over Yourself, Decide to Lead: Insights from Hard Lessons Learned.*

I had to chuckle when Strickland wrote, "You took the first step, you know you are a bad leader." What a powerful statement.

<u>Wayne Strickland's Advice to Bad Leaders</u>

"Many times, in a person's career, they reach a fork in the road and they must decide if they take the easy path or the more challenging one. Most people take the easy path and tell themselves they are taking the tougher path, and they use that to justify their decisions. Then if they don't get to where they want to go, they play the victim card.

The first step in turning a leadership career around is knowing that you have problems. The next is getting someone to help you understand what behaviors are causing you the biggest problem. This might be someone in HR, an Executive Coach, or a smart cir-cle of friends. No matter who you turn to, you need feedback.

At my biggest fork in the road, in my career, I had to make some very tough choices. At one of my lowest points in my personal and professional life, I made the decision to listen to those most important to me, and to make hard decisions to change the way I worked. I changed my behaviors. My ideas and energy and drive were all great, but my behaviors were not.

To make this simple, imagine 3 columns with these headings: Good behaviors, bad behaviors and derailers. [Note from the author: A leadership derailer is a leader who stands in the way of progress and innovation.] The first two columns are clear: they are things that make you better and things that make you worse. The third column are the behaviors that get you fired, lose your station in life or both.

At 50 years old, divorced, paying alimony, a house payment, with [two] kids in college, and one more on the way to college, and living in a small little student apartment and alternating between hamburger and tuna helper each night I finally listened. I was ready to not be in this place anymore.

I actually believed that some of my behaviors were a strength when in fact they were the number one reasons why I was stalled in my career and having a do over in my personal life.

It took me over a year just to accept that they were actually bad behaviors and then a long time to consistently, if not, permanently, eliminate them. This was no easy task and many days I still debated with myself if this was a good or bad behavior.

Fast forward to today. I found the perfect partner and she and I have been married almost 10 years. We have a big, merged family and my career had a big growth spurt and finished my corporate work life at the top my game.

But this all started with being honest about my own behaviors and then doing something about it."

Chapter Seven:
Innovative Leadership

Leadership requires creativity, innovation, and embracing the creativity and innovation of followers.

Far too often, we cling to what is familiar, even if what we cling to is known to be inadequate. Most large groups are governed by the law of inertia: if it takes the determination to change something, nothing will change. As a leader, you must search out opportunities to change, grow, innovate, and improve.

There is no reward without risk, so you must be willing to experiment, take risks, and learn from any mistakes. Ask questions, even if you fear the answers. Start with the question, "Why?" Why are things the way they are? Why do we do things the way we do? Please do not forget that when an organization is in transition, so are the employees. Ibarra et al. (2010:666) define transition as being "in the process of leaving one thing without having fully left it, and at the same time of entering something else, without being fully a part of it."

Think Outside the Box

A *paradigm* is an established model or structure. Sometimes they work quite well, but often they are inadequate or even counterproductive. Sometimes it is necessary to "think outside the box" and break the paradigm. Do not be afraid to ask the question "Why?" Ask questions of your followers, employees, customers, and former leaders. Answers and ideas can be found in the least likely places. Often the lowest ranking persons in an organization can tell you exactly what is wrong because they see it daily from their vantage points.

Inclusiveness should not be considered "outside of the box," yet it is. The more open you are to hearing input from those in every level and position, the more information you will have and the emotionally invest your staff will be.

Developing Your Inner Innovator

Innovation is more than just improving on a process or procedure; it is a total redirection or restructuring based upon stated goals and research. While it can be helpful to adapt an outdated procedure or task to today's standards, often the procedure itself is the problem, not the manner in which one implements the procedure. Innovators reverse engineer policies and procedures based on the new vision and goals, working from the target backward, rather than from the status quo looking forward.

To be clear, not all innovative strategies will be feasible or cost effective. Requiring an entirely new computerized network and infrastructure, for example, may cost hundreds of thousands of dollars and produce little-improved efficiency over the old one; however, if you do not start thinking "outside the box," you will miss many valuable solutions that can and will work.

Change should never be made simply for the sake of change. Change can be exciting, but it can also be unnerving and difficult for employees. Constant change causes frustration.

Reminder: Leadership requires creativity, innovation, and embracing the creativity and innovation of followers.

Moreover, if you seem to change too many things too often, you will lose respect, as your followers perceive you do not really know what you are doing; so be sure to plan your innovations carefully. There should be solid evidence that a new way of doing things is likely to work before you invest money and everyone's time.

Keep focused on the goals and be willing to break the rules, if rule-breaking is required. Just make sure they really need to be broken and you do not break something that needs to keep working! With proper research and planning, you can dare to be bold!

Food for thought: This question arises from the Hill et al. (2010) article. Leadership, according to the authors, is necessary for innovation. Innovation is necessary for outstanding performance (perceived as being "beyond customer imagination." The authors call Mandela a social innovator because he led from behind. He was a shepherd who understood the need to push, motivate, engage, protect, and forecast events. With that said there must be a context, climate, and cohesiveness conducive to a foundation for innovation. I like that the authors said that protégés are born but are made by their social interactions. Is it possible to have innovation without leadership? I say, No. What say you?

Seeing Room for Improvement

A strong vision does not lend itself to mediocrity. A drive to excellence always seeks improvement. If you accept 95% efficiency as a goal, the efficiency will inevitably slip to 90%. If that's considered "good enough," it will become hard to keep it above 85% and so on. A vision is a goal that someone or an organization must strive to achieve. A leader must be a visionary who strives for excellence and is uncomfortable with complacency or mediocrity.

Goals that are not realistic or attainable are dreams. Followers of dreamers, rather than a visionary-leader, will simply give up trying altogether, becoming dispirited and demoralized in the process. If 95% of people fail to meet a standard, then that standard is likely too high and must be changed. On the other hand, the bar must not be set so low that little or no effort is required to meet it. Those on your team will thrive when challenged – not strained or provoked. The work environment is a place for personal growth and development. A leader must be aware of the appropriate goals set to the appropriate timeline, in order to challenge the employees without causing them to feel unbearably overwhelmed or fatigued.

Based on your vision, set high goals that are attainable but with some degree of difficulty, and reward those who meet the goals. [This will also help kep the antsy follower feeling challenged and engaged. There is always someone anxious for promotion or who needs to be constantly challenged.] If a large number of followers are meeting the goal, raise the target. If only a very few are meeting it, lower it somewhat. Be flexible and aware. If the group is under-performing, consider whether the problem is caused by a goal set to high, lack of level appropriate leadershiip, miscommunication (or lack of) related to the goal and targeted achievement, or the individuals tasked with accomplishing the goal are not the right fit.

Investigate any potential bottlenecks that might be stifling progress and resolve them. Talk to your followers about possible solutions. The people who actually do the work are far more likely to be able to tell you why they are having difficulty accomplishing a task than their supervisors. The gossipy office member – bottleneck. The disgruntled manager that was passed over for a promotion – bottleneck. Inadequate technology – bottleneck. Unstaffing or appropiately trained staff – bottleneck. Of course, always make sure that you are not the bottleneck. Self-actualization and assessment are important. If you see that you are the one holding up progress, great, now figure out why!

Lobbying for Change

Change within an organization must be inspired not forced. Leading in the midst of change or a need for change requires a person with the communication skills necessary to influence, excite and inspire participation in the vision. Whether to rip the proverbial band-aid off quickly or peel it back slowly, in the end, the outcome will be the same some sore spots, some healing areas, and a sharp sting. Inevitably you will need to tap into your gift for persuasion or use diplomacy and negotiate. You may need to persuade a stubborn or reluctantly progressive boss or combat a corporate culture that pushes back against what you are trying to do. You will likely need to demonstrate your rationale and present evidence for why the requested change needs to occur.

Do your due diligence before any meetings. Do not let anyone catch you unprepared (or in a lie). Be sure to take time to assess the situation and present all of your findings in a professionally styled yet brief report. Preferably, a report with easy to follow charts or graphs. Know your audience. Present only information that they absolutely need to know and definitely want to know. All other information can be put into a handout for future reading. Facts are important but should not overwhelm the listeners. Remain anchored in the temporal flow of change. Show them the past, pre-change (present), change (implementation), and post-change expectations. Acknowledge that there may be anxiety associated with change. Yet, help transform that anxiety into excitement.

If you are advocating your own group of followers, the same applies. You will likely want to revolutionize a shift in the corporate culture. Perhaps you are the manager of an office or shop filled with unmotivated staff. Undoubtedly, you as the leader will need to implement any changes slowly (in phases), an audacious change could create animosity and mistrust. That is why it is important to remember that when you react to the numbers (data, P & L, stock, etc.) you are doing something that will cause your followers to react to you. Some say that people will follow you if you are enthusiastic. I say people follow authentic enthusiasm. We live in a world of B.S. singers who can smell B.S. a mile away.

Maintaining control in a meeting

In addressing change or challenges within a particular context, meetings are inevitable. We all seem to have a love-hate relation-ship with meetings. If we are leading the meeting, most often we feel the meeting is necessary. If anyone else is leading the meeting, we start to groan, moan, and figure out how to be productive doing other work while in the meeting. However, in the instance where a change occurs, and we were not given notice, we become upset that we were not included in the meetings. Your followers feel much the same way.

HERE ARE A FEW TRICKS TO A SUCCESSFUL MEETING:

- Answer questions but use them as a base to return to the main reason for the meeting – communicating the strategic plan and evolving vision.

- Be realistic about the current financial positioning, targets/goals, and timelines.

- Clearly explain the need for collective responsibility.

- Come prepared with talking points. There is no "hot seat" when you are prepared with a plan for productivity.

- Do not allow followers to make leadership solely accountable for the overall success. Remind them that success is a collective effort. While doing so, do not be afraid to take ownership for failures (even if it was before your term).

- Do not be hesitant to disagree. Proceed cautiously.

- Do not be led by the questions. Answer questions in such a way that your answers lead subsequent questions. Anticipate follow-up questions.

- Foster "buy-in." Now is not time for meeting for the sake of meeting.

- Let the audience know the plan for answering a complex question. For example, "To answer that question, I am going to break it into three parts." This will prepare the listeners for a lengthy answer. At the same time, it slows the pace of the questioning.

- Listen to negatives; but, refocus/redirect to the positive outcomes and plans.

- Only give as much information as is needed. Do not overwhelm people with extraneous information or stray from the central theme of the meeting.

- Pay homage to the past but be realistic about the impact past decisions had on the current situation.

- Present the vision as a collective vision rather than an individual vision.

- Reassurance is more important than correction at times.

- Remind followers that change is inevitable. The type of change, however, can be controlled. Focus on the future while being informed by the past. Change can be reactive, but it must be proactive.

- Start the meeting by reading or displaying the mission to help focus and refocus the conversations and reminding attendees that all discussions and decisions must be shaped by or linked to the vision and mission.

- Transparency does not mean they will like the answer. The goal of transparency is to make the hearer responsible for the information they receive. Or to say – Now that you know, what are you going to do with the information?

- Use personal weaknesses to disarm and add levity to the meeting. This communicates that while there is clear leadership, leaders have flaws similar in some ways to those of the followers. It reduces the gap between the leadership and followers while maintaining respect.

- Validate the feelings of concerned attendees without validating erroneous information or perceptions. Maintain a business focus when validating feelings to avoid ranting and whining.

- When an attendee is determined to pose a chain of questions, regain control by relinquishing control. Ask the person for a solution. This will most likely halt the seemingly endless flow of questions, and communicate the shared responsibility and foster "buy-in."

- Bonus 1: Be personal, direct, and unwavering.

- Bonus 2: No matter who you are speaking to, speak to everyone listening.

- Bonus 3: Solicit input while communicating that input does not mean final say.

Practical Illustration

David entered his leader's office. Kaitlyn welcomed him inside, and the two of them sat down. David asked, "I was wondering why you wanted to see me. I hope nothing's wrong."

Kaitlyn said, "Absolutely not. Things are going wonderfully. You met your sales goals for this quarter, and as a whole, we're meeting the goals we set."

David nodded, not understanding why he'd been called to her office.

Kaitlyn said. "The best time to plan for the future is when things are going well. We need to plan our next step. Now that we've met this goal, we need to challenge ourselves with another one. I called you here today so that you could help make a measurable, attainable goal for our team."

David was more than happy to pitch in and give his input. This helped Kaitlyn build a relationship with her employee, and challenging them with another goal also set an example for her staff, too.

The only man who makes no mistakes is the man who never does anything.

Theodore Roosevelt

Chapter Eight:
Empowering Others to Act

As mentioned before, you cannot do your followers' work for them. Besides, if you do their work, why are they getting paid? You have your work to do. This is the ultimate goal of the Hersey-Blanchard Situational Leadership model: to develop your followers to the point where you can delegate tasks without a lot of oversight.

To be a true leader, you must enable others to act responsibly and not encourage bad worker habits by compensating for them or overlooking them. Negative, ineffective, or domineering leadership can have a huge impact on the trajectory of an organization due to its implications for the followers themselves (Gooty, 2010). At the same time, you cannot berate a follower for trying hard but making an honest mistake. The goal of a leader is to empower others to work. To the extent that you can do this is the extent that you will be successful.

Encouraging Growth in Others

A positive attitude is essential to encouragement. No one likes to fail and many take it very personally. While failure should never be rewarded, an understanding attitude and positive outlook can work wonders. A child only learns to walk by falling many times. The focus is not on the fall, but on getting up. The goal is to walk...then to run.

Meeting with an employee one-on-one is important to positive motivation. Here again, you must use the power of listening. Avoid blame when something goes wrong and focus on the reason for the failure. You may learn someone needs more training, more self-confidence, or more freedom. You may learn someone does not have the tools needed to be successful. You will never know if you do not ask questions and listen – or worse, if you berate someone for failure.

If someone is willfully defiant, then feel free to be stern and resolute. Take disciplinary action if necessary and document the conversation. If you allow someone to be defiant or lazy out of a misplaced concern for his or her feelings, you will be performing a great injustice against the rest who are working hard. In most cases, people really do want to do a good job, and they have a sense of pride when they meet a challenge.

Creating Mutual Respect

You will never be worthy of respect if you do not give respect. Respect should be given to everyone at all levels unless they deliberately do something to lose that respect.

You need to build respect in other ways as well. Be visible to your followers. Show them you are available and interested in knowing everything about what they do. Develop and demonstrate your knowledge of the organization and details of the product, service, or operation. If you are perceived as being knowledgeable and can answer questions, you will not only earn respect but will motivate others to learn as well.

The Importance of Trust

Much of the current leadership development industry has lost touch with, minimizes, or negates the role and the importance of followers as advisors and resources. The growing focus on leadership development does not consider the communication and connection of the leader to followers.

Respect inevitably leads to trust. Do what you say and say what you mean. Under-promising and over-delivering can help manage expectations. If you are given a task you know will take you one hour, say you "should" have it done in two hours. You never know when you'll get a phone call that eats into your time or when an emergency may pop up. If you get done in less than two hours, you will be perceived as a hero. If not, you can call and apologize that it will be "a little later" without much trouble because you said you should have it done. You did not promise that you would have it done. If people feel they can rely on you, they will trust you.

Also, let people know that you are not asking them to do anything you would not do yourself, or have not done in the past. Work hard and be seen working hard. If you come in early and see others who are there early as well, stop by and simply mention that fact positively. A simple word of recognition will go a long way to earning respect. Without respect, you will never have loyalty and without loyalty, you cannot trust your followers. Without mutual trust and respect, you cannot accomplish great things.

Remember: while your people need to be able to trust you, you need to build them up to the level where you can also trust them.

Celebrate group and individual accomplishments (apart from your own). Implement goal setting and benchmarking remaining open to the ideas of others within and outside of the group/organization. It is essential to the organization that you make sure there is liberty – as a sense of freedom – for a follower to provide input, but do not relinquish your power to make the decision whether or not there is consensus. Recognize that there is no leader without the followers – work together not lead separately. This will help you build mutual trust.

Practical Illustration

Adam worked on building respect with his staff from the beginning. He came back from lunch, and he waved to one of his followers, Catherine. He stopped by her cubicle and asked her, "How are things going?"

Catherine sighed and said, "I've been trying to be innovative about this next product launch like you said, but I'm really struggling with finding a new angle."

Adam said, "Is that the same one due by the end of the week?"

"Yes. Do you think you could get me some help with brainstorming?"

Adam assigned another follower to partner with Catherine that he knew excelled at fresh ideas and innovation. Because he showed respect to his followers, they trusted him to let them know how projects were going, good or bad. The problem was addressed, in a quick and effective manner.

Those who fail to plan, plan to fail.

Anonymous

Have a 'Do Not Do List': Brian Liam

Brian Lim

Founder and CEO of iHeartRaves and INTO THE AM

https://www.iheartraves.com/

https://www.intotheam.com/

Brian Lim is the Founder and CEO of *iHeartRaves* and *INTO THE AM*. They are curators of all over print clothing and world leaders in festival fashion. They currently gross over $20M a year and been featured in the Inc. 5000, four years in a row. Mr. Lim, and he had this to say:

"Make sure your ideas align with your mission statement. If they don't, move on. I believe in the importance of having a "Do Not Do" list. In the beginning, I was the guy that tried to do everything on my own. As I've grown, I've definitely learned there's a lot of value in networking and building relationships. The relationships that I've formed are what's opening doors for the future. Learning the art of delegating tasks has helped me today I wish I knew that in the early years. Having processes and procedures in place is very important for developing these traits in the world of business."

*Special thanks to Brandon Chopp, the Digital Manager for iHeartRaves and INTO THE AM, for facilitating this connection and content.

What Does It Take?

Lisa Sansom is the founder of LVS Consulting, a boutique consulting firm that helps to build positive organizations. In these roles, Ms. Sansom shares positive psychology tools and techniques with her clients through speaking, corporate training and coaching. She works with clients in education from preschool through to higher education, and also many corporate and not-for-profit clients. Ms. Sansom obtained her MBA from the Rotman School of

Management, and earned her coaching accreditation from Adler International Learning / OISE-UT. In addition, she holds an Honours Bachelor of Arts from the University of Waterloo and a Bachelor of Education from Brock University. She completed her MAPP (Master of Applied Positive Psychology) from the University of Pennsylvania in 2010.

LVS Consulting - Creating Positive Organizations

"The best leaders, as far as I can tell in my experience, are those who are strengths-based. What do I mean by that? They know their own strengths and they lead from their strengths, and know what they are not good at, acknowledge their weaknesses and craft a strong team around them to overcome those weaknesses. These leaders also focus on the strengths of others, and while they coach and mentor to grow and develop others around them (not just those who report to them, but everyone around them), they also know how to support those strengths in others and position those other people for success and growth. These top leaders care from their heart about the people around them, and they work actively and passionately to make the workplace a place of thriving and meaning. While they certainly keep their eyes on the "bottom line" (however that might be defined by their business and industry), they never lose track of the people side of the equation, and they know that the "soft stuff" is really the "hard stuff". These leaders are always driving themselves to be better, to do better and to learn more - they are on a constant quest of self-development, and they engage with others in that learning. There is no one "personality type" that makes for the best leadership style or approach - anyone who wants to can learn to be a successful leader."

Kristin Halpin Perry, a former Chief Human Resources Officer, has been transforming company cultures and their leaders to be business savvy and compassionate, resilient and flexible, and most importantly, integrity-driven, for 20+ years all around the globe. The Veraz approach to understanding where everyone is coming from, which has helped her wrangle ragtag groups into legendary teams, while making sure everyone from C-Suite executives to bright-eyed interns feel like part of the whole community.

Kristin, as she prefers, is the Founder and Chief Consultant-in-Arms at Veraz Consulting.

verazconsulting.com

kristin@verazconsulting.com

"If there is one thing I've learned throughout my career is that successful leaders come from all walks of life. Whether you're an introvert who quietly leads or a dynamic extrovert who naturally draws in a crowd. The leaders who people respect and follow the most model behaviors that demonstrate mutual respect, cultivate ideas and creativity, demonstrates fortitude, while leading with ingenuity and integrity. The simple truth is to be grounded with who you are as a person and surround yourself with diverse styles and ideas. Integrity combined with humility and courage, however that shows up, will lead you on the path of success."

Using her natural talent and extensive training and experience, Kristen gave us a brief anecdote about an "introverted CEO."

"I was hired as a CHRO (Chief HR Officer) at a tech start-up company for the automotive industry. They were exploding with growth and needed me to come in and help bring in some infrastructure, but not too much, where it might stifle their unique culture.

The CEO was a gifted technologist who also liked to mountain bike, snowboard and rock climb, which clearly demonstrated his high level of adrenaline. He cared deeply about people but didn't like the attention that CEO's typically receive especially with the media, which was knocking on their doors any chance they could get to find out why everyone wanted to work there. What made him a successful leader was that he encouraged transparency, hired people around him that brought innovative thoughts, instilled mutual trust and made you feel like you were special and apart of the team no matter what level you were at. He was grounded with who he was and created a safe environment for others to follow. He brought a quiet strength to the company that people admired, which motivated them to go beyond what they ever thought they could do in their life and in their career."

Dr. Susan O'Malley, former emergency room physician, entrepreneur and author, shares strategies she learned under life and death conditions and combines them with stories from the trenches to help executives and entrepreneurs conquer their business challenges.

Drawing on her own experiences of personal and professional setbacks and challenges, she outlines strategies that transformed her from college drop-out and secretary to emergency room doctor and entrepreneur in her book *Tough Cookies Don't Crumble: Turn SetBacks into Success.*

www.susanomalleymd.com

drsusan@susanomalleymd.com

"A successful leader knows that even though they are in charge, they're not the smartest person in the room. There are many attributes that make a leader successful, one being accepting responsibility for leadership. Once you accept responsibility for being the leader, your primary objective is to bring out the leader in everyone – your teammates, your spouse and your children.

Leadership is not making decisions and telling people what to do. It's helping other people achieve their fullest potential. If people fear the leader they will strive to protect themselves, if people love the leader they will strive to protect the leader.

And your goal is to create an environment where people will contribute and be productive. Leadership is similar to parenting because your goal as a parent is not to raise a child who will listen to everything you say; instead your goal as a parent is to raise a leader."

Scott Greenberg helps leaders and franchisees grow their business. He has given presentations in all 50 U.S. states and throughout the world to clients such McDonalds, Allstate, RE/MAX and the U.S. Air Force. For more than a decade, he was a multi-unit franchisee with Edible Arrangements. His operation won the *"Best Customer Service"* and *"Manager of the Year"* awards out of more than 1000 locations worldwide. More information at ww.scottgreenberg.com

"The key to effective leadership is to think of yourself as the ultimate servant. You exist to serve your team and elevate their performance. This is counter-intuitive for leaders who are driven by ego. They focus on building themselves rather than building their organization. My employees understood they didn't work for me; they worked for our customers. If a customer was upset and I wasn't there to help, my employees were trained to ask not what I would want, but what does the customer want? What will make them happy? More importantly, what will bring them back? As long as those questions drove their decision, they'd always have my support. Good leaders make others feel important without concern for how they look. Let your employees be the star and let them work for the customers."

John Barker has 20 years providing technology consulting providing outsource Chief Information Officer services and leading-edge cybersecurity tools with his company Attollo Systems.

jbarker@attollosystems.com

www.attollosystems.com

Barker says, a leader must be "calm under pressure."

"Company leaders are typically easy to work with when things are going smoothly. A sign of a truly successful leader is to keep that same demeanor when more stressful situations arise. A calm presence in the face of trouble will get passed along to all other company employees. A sense of "we've got this" will take hold and everyone will battle thru the adversity.

'Leaders' that get panicky, indecisive, or worse angry will breed that same sentiment throughout the organization, and the likelihood of the problem getting worse grows. Team members may see their empowerment taken away for no good reason. Then the leader becomes a bottleneck slowing progress.

A leader that can maintain a calming presence still allows their team to function as they normally would in the good times but may provide more assistance without becoming a burden. Leaders need to realize that their staff will begin to mimic their emotional state. *When a project isn't working as planned or an unknown risk pops up out of nowhere, take a deep breath, remain calm, and tell your team 'we're going to crush it'. "*

Steven Benson is the Founder and CEO of Badger Maps, the #1 route planner for field salespeople. After receiving his MBA from Stanford, Steve's career has been in field sales with companies like IBM, Autonomy, and Google – becoming Google Enterprise's Top Performing Salesperson in the World in 2009. In 2012, Steve founded Badger Maps to help field salespeople be more successful. He has also been selected as one of the Top 40 Most Inspiring Leaders in Sales Lead Management.

www.badgermapping.com

Facebook: www.facebook.com/badgermaps

YouTube: www.youtube.com/user/BadgerMapping

"In my opinion empathy is one of the most important skills great leaders have. Without the ability to use your mind to put yourself inside the shoes of another person and understand where they are coming from, you can't really connect with people. Leaders who fail to empathize often create negative work experiences, because they don't appreciate the impact of the way they set things up, the cultural norms they create, or how they treat people.

Leaders can quickly and easily increase their empathy by consciously thinking about how their employees feel, and imagining themselves being in the position that their employees are in. They should also consider how the environment they create would make them feel if they want to create a great environment to work in.

When leading a team, it's also important to be a great motivator and help all employees perform at their best. Great leaders are able to help them understand the big picture, so they can connect their success back to the success of the business. They are great coaches and show their employees that they care about them, their career, and their future by giving them the information, training, and knowledge to be successful."

Deborah Sweeney is the CEO of MyCorporation.com which provides online legal filing services for entrepreneurs and businesses, startup bundles that include corporation and LLC formation, registered agent services, DBAs, and trademark and copyright filing services.

MyCorporation.com

Deborah@deborahsweeney.com

"Many small business owners have difficulty letting go of their business and delegating the work to their team. When they do let go, they often try to micromanage and control the projects and assignments everyone else is working on. My best advice for improvement is to follow the quote 'Lead from within, not from out front.' Empower and trust your team to keep the business humming without you micromanaging. If you try to run everything yourself, you'll eventually crash and burn."

Adam Cole is an author, educator, and gifted performer. Adam was educated at Oberlin College and at the Georgia State University School of Music. At the General Music for Middle School in Fulton County, he served as Chair. After serving in public education for 12 years, he decided co-found the Grant Park Academy of the Arts with Katherine Moore. Adam also worked as a Project Manager for the Georgia Department of Education to assist with their revisions of the State Standards for the Arts. www.grantparkarts.com

"Being a good leader means putting the mission first, the one that your organization is committed to, and keeping it above your personal desires for gain or control. It means modeling optimal choices for how to accomplish it, so those working with you and under you feel a sense of cohesion. Finally, it means knowing when to push and when to listen.

If you want to set yourself up to be a good leader, my advice would be to have yourself as together of a person as possible, know your own issues, and ensure that [those issues] don't distract from your role as leader. Do whatever it takes to become a present, stable, open person. Therapy, self-help tools, or just a good friend (or spouse!) that can set you straight - you've got to have resources in your life that can keep you from living too much in your own head and missing the important things. [Have some people who are willing to tell you that you are wrong or help you discover your flaws in a safe and compassionate (even loving) way.] I seek di-versity in the opinions of people I listen to. Different walks of life, different skill sets. It's too easy to get caught up in your own little world and not realize you're missing opportunities in a bigger one."

17 Traits of a Successful Leader: Wayne Strickland

Wayne Strickland

Business Consultant, Author, Speaker

waynestricklandspeaking.com

Hopefully, you recall Mr. Strickland's background from Chapter Six. Briefly, he had a successful 25-year Vice President at Hallmark Cards. Mr. Strickland has extraordinary experiences to share from his successes and failures, which have informed his approach to building a competitive culture with enlightened leadership.

Mr. Strickland provided a wealth of information when asked, "What is the Personality of a Successful Leader?"

"Successful leaders have the following personality traits. These are the traits of great leaders that are successful time and time again-- no matter the job or industry.

1. They are always growing professionally; they add new skills not more ego.

2. The are never satisfied with their results, never matter how good they are.

3. They focus and drive the big ideas that will move the business forward and avoid getting trapped in the smaller projects that don't matter

4. They understand the corporate political landscape and navigate it but never try to change it, because it will not change

5. They understand that the culture they create their organizations is much more important that the strategy they develop and dedicate time to making the culture healthy.

6. They are always recruiting the best talent and moving their best people to better jobs.

7. They lead organizations that everyone wants to work in because you get better.

8. They have balance in their lives and find the places outside of work that bring them joy.

9. They take care of their health. In fact, they prioritize their health.

10. They understand the competitive marketplace intimately and they rarely get surprised by new ideas in the marketplace.

11. The build great teams and with people who are look different, think different, have different skills and demands open debate on the tough issues.

12. They are decisive and make sure everyone understands what the decision is, why they made it and what it means for each group or individual on the team.

13. They operate against a set of quantifiable metrics that informs them if they are meeting the important milestones that will lead them to their goals.

14. They are sensitive to their people but strict with the strategy.

15. They are great listeners and spend more time asking questions than talking.

16. They are great communicators and know what to say, to each group, and when to say it. And they repeat in over and over again.

17. The best leaders are just a little insecure... but never show it."

Chapter Nine:
Church Leadership
by Pastor Loretta L. Stevens

Pastor Loretta L. Stevens, a native of Newark, NJ, is the Senior Pastor and President/Chief Executive Officer of Community House of Prayer, Inc. She is a gifted and skilled leader, who leads with a heart.

Prior to my husband and pastor, the late Elder John G. Stevens' death in August 2005, I believed heading up a ministry or committee was leadership at its best. Involvement in the ministry afforded me the opportunity to initiate programs, execute ideas, teach Bible Study, head up women's and youth groups, be a community outreach representative, etc. However, I had to reevaluate the leadership role after I became a pastor. There is a distinct difference between a leadership role and a leader in charge. The overall vision for the church is given to the leader/pastor "in charge" and disseminated among those appointed in leadership roles. The vision is given to the Pastor and the ministries will align itself within the vision of the pastor.

The church is an organism, a form of life composed with many mutually interdependent parts that maintain various vital processes1. I'm sure this is a strange way to describe a house of worship, a place that facilitates life transformation, soul salvation and renewal. The primary focus of the church is sharing the Word of God that people might receive Christ as their Savior, be redeemed, live a righteous life and ultimately spend eternity in heaven. A successful ministry is concerned about the mind, body, and soul of all, however, at the same time there is the business side.

We cringe when the church is referred to as a Business. The Church is unique from a secular business because all (from A-Z) should be or supposed to be focused on the development of the church and the spiritual growth of the congregation. Yes, many of the same rules apply in running a secular business as in the church. Similarities, in the growth of the establishment, increases in revenue, budgeting, strategy, vision, and relationships are obvious in both. The Pastor/leader in charge must understand when too much emphasis is placed on the "secular", in doing so, the church and the body of Christ will suffer because God's House should be used and developed for Godly purposes. There are many facets behind the overall operational functionality of the Church including but not limited to:

- building acquisition/maintenance,
- finance/ budgeting
- fundraising
- outreach and evangelism
- ordinances of the church,
- community involvement and recognition
- Christian education/schools
- many ministries, counseling, music, youth programs

... and the list is exhaustive to say the least. This is extremely important; the pastor must oversee each operation without losing sight of the overall mission and purpose of the ministry. The principal function of the church is to nurture, teach and encourage all through the Word of God, reach the lost and heal the hurting. So often the business side takes precedent over the spiritual and the primary focus is lost.

CHURCH MEETINGS

The church business meeting is essential. When conducting the meeting, I preface the meeting with the following statement "How many of you have the Holy Spirit", I'll wait for a show of hands (of course all hands are raised), "great" I'll say, "if all have the Holy Spirit, we should be able to conduct God's business in grace and harmony. Disagreement on the topic discussed is ok, however, we do not have to be disagreeable, now let's pray." I have found in the ten years since I have been pastor, we have never left angry after a church meeting, but rejoicing, thanking God for success, shaking hands and greeting one another. A leader must always have control of the temperament of the meeting, knowing how to put out fires before they start. Listen to the advice, opinions, and suggestions of those attending the meeting. You will find that the ideas of others are considered necessary for the following reasons:

1. Ideas from others offer the attendees the confidence of knowing that their opinions are important enough to be heard or considered. If the suggestion is not used, make them feel your appreciation for their input.

2. I have found that the benefit of suggestions can add to and/or bring in points of interest that never crossed my mind.

3. Understand that an opinion from others does not go against your management/leadership skills - it enhances them, you have actually connected with the inner thoughts, enthusiasm, and creativity of those at the meeting.

4. Be confident in your presentation of new ideas if you expect to get a good result. Think of possible questions that may come up in reference to your ideas and be prepared to answer them.

DELEGATE

Delegate, Delegate, Delegate! A great leader will delegate, doing so will free them up to concentrate or focus on the vision God has given them for the ministry. I must admit that most pastors may only have a gift of preaching; however, church administration, outreach, etc. may not be his/her forte'. A pastor's job is a 24/7 calling, not a career, a calling from God to do the work for God which includes preaching, teaching, counseling, and hospital visitations among other things. The busy schedule, plus sermon preparation is enough to overwhelm a pastor, why should you take on more. Delegate the women's/men's ministry, children's ministry, feeding/clothing ministry, etc.

My first two years as pastor, I tried to head up every ministry of the church. I sincerely believed that my presence was needed at every meeting, my input was the oil that made the machine work, and if I did not assist in doing the work, the church would fall apart. I even wrote Christmas and Easter plays! After a few years of that, I was absolutely exhausted. I asked God for help and He basically said, "help yourself to those in the congregation that are ready, willing, and able to head functions in which they can use the gift that I gave them". That was an eye opener! Pastor's suffer from 'burn-out' because they fail to delegate. As an effective leader, evaluate your programs, pray and ask God to lead you to those qualified to take some of the burdens off your shoulders. You may have the gift of expounding on the Word of God, but you may not have the gift or time to write plays.

DEACONS/TRUSTEES/PASTORS ASSISTANTS

In the Apostle books of the New Testament, Paul realized he needed help. He reached out to Peter, Erastus, Silas, Titus, Timothy, Lydia, etc. to aid him in the ministry. God has given us pastoral assistants, deacons, and trustees to take care of the burden of financing, fundraising, church/land acquisition etc. A deacon and associate minister CAN also give you a break every now and then from preaching or teaching. Let them exercise their gift. A good leader will not be threatened by the assistance of others, but appreciative for their support. Ask them to visit a hospital, jail, nursing home, you may be pleasantly surprised at their willingness to help.

RELATIONSHIPS

Building healthy relationships within the congregation is vital. Most people come as a result of an invitation from a family member or friend. The visitor may be looking for a place of acceptance, what better place than the house of God. Foster relationships within the ministry to make members and visitors feel they are in a place where they can feel accepted and encouraged to grow spiritually. It is important that each member have an experience of inclusion and leave the church service feeling uplifted and equipped to face the challenges of life's encounters.

Ministries offering marriage, singles, family activities, and counseling are very effective in strengthening the home, which actually strengthens the church. It is also a good idea and important to build relationships with local businesses, local government and the community to aid the church in name recognition, resources and support when needed.

CONCLUDING THOUGHTS

As leaders, we must understand that it's not a one man/woman show. We need people for a successful outcome. Fostering an environment of inclusion, acceptance, and creativity will yield many benefits. When people are offering their time, participation, willingness to work and increased attendance, the ministry will grow in spirit and membership.

➢ Delegate, put God first, pray about who should lead programs within the ministry, have checkpoints and trust God to give you and them the knowledge needed to complete the task.

➢ Again, the church is a place of worship, a place where the spiritual needs of the people are the primary focus. In keeping the will of God as your priority, God's favor will flow, and the ministry will be a success.

Chapter Ten:
Diversity with Inclusion

Groups consist of people caught in a battle between the need or desire for autonomy and the desire to fulfill social obligations. Diversity of beliefs and ideas are just as important as diversity of culture. A team's dynamic is indicative of current performance and predictive of future performance. As a good leader you are most likely or will be tasked with building a team including adding new team members, shifting current members to other roles or teams, removing members, and creating and managing new or additional teams.

Remember, the successful transformation of an organization is aided by gender and cultural diversity, which provide "slices of genius" or a broad spectrum of thoughts, innovative ideas, and perspectives (Nohria & Khurana, 2010; Hill et al., 2010). If diversity were truly embedded in organizational human resource processes, there would not be a question as to whether diversity and inclusion should be considered, only analyzing the best ways to ensure both are maintained. Likely, considering the global climate, you will be working within the context of an organization with a new or increased focus on diversity, cultural sensitivity, real rather than symbolic inclusiveness, and reducing work-place anxiety related to the increase in personnel from diverse groups.

We cannot consider it a stretch to see how minorities, women, or locals can consider the D&I plan to be as focused on compliance rather than a business opportunity. Diversity is not about checking the box. Diversity is the core to your bottom line, productivity, growth, expansion, increased client or donor base, and overall sustainability of the institution. The "check the box" approach to diversity is counterproductive. For instance, In America, a Black woman can fulfill both the gender and the African-American requirement – leaving out Black males who have an extremely high unemployment rate – especially for higher paying and highly visible positions. There are no complaints from me about the increasing number of Black women in C-suite and Board positions. There is a sense of sadness to know that when an organization fills the role with a Black woman, some may do so out of prejudice toward the Black male or out of their need to prove their commitment to women and racial diversity with a single new-hire or promotion.

Back to the idea of diverse ideas rather than just diverse cultures. Innovation is grown from one's experiences in life. An organization will become stifled if the majority of their decision-making and creative employees are from a similar background, race aside. If all of your decision-makers and creatives are from suburban, middle-income, two-parent homes, that went to the best state college on scholarship, then that is the limit of your innovation. Innovation is born through travel, hardship, networking, family, background, education, and so much more. You need a team that has one eye with many lenses rather than a team all seeing the context through the same lens.

When working to implement a more diverse group, consider the following objectives:

1. Maintain or exceed diversity and inclusion ratios within groups and across the organization.

2. Implement a plan for diversity and inclusion once the organization is positioned to hire or rehire personnel. This does not mean that diversity should go on the back-burner to that of profit or sustainability. Diversity is a driving force of those things. However, diversity can be a costly endeavor for an organization lacking diversity. As such, you need to create a strategic plan specifically for diversity so that the organization can be financially and contextually positioned and ready for diversity.

3. Retrain personnel on the importance of embracing differences – especially given shrinking numbers.

4. Create and meet the target number of women, minorities, and locals in upper-tier leadership positions (positions of influence or power). Using National Census data, local demographic information, and industry best practices.

Steps for meeting the four objectives:

o **Seek** input from clients, employees, volunteers, other leaders, community organizations, vendor, suppliers, governments, and locales as to the best plan for restructuring to mitigate devastation to the local economy.

o **Add** diversity to the group advising the restructuring process. I once worked with a non-profit organization that sought a more diverse board of directors. They did everything contextually correct. They even formed a sub-committee to address diversity. The committee was made up of mostly White males and one White female and all were within the financially comfortable in post-retirement demographic. That organization is still working on diversity and cannot understand why they do not have it. As the organization begins to fade, I hope they revisit the notes from our meeting.

o **Assess** the current employment ratio within groups, and then across the organization.

o **Consider** the needs of the future - consider age, gender, race, and nationality. What will the future client or donor look like? What are the future expectations of the job? Who are the inspirational voices of the generation? What will it take to be a future leader in the organization?

o **Increase** focus on all forms of diversity. Diversity is more than what people see. Again, diversity of ideas, prospective, experiences, work experience, education, etc. are all important to leading a successful team.

o **Align** the restructuring process to consider the organizational definitions of diversity and inclusion – in a measurable way. Practical not theoretical changes.

○ **Reconsider** the economic impact diversity and lack of diversity will have on the profitability or all groups (upstream and downstream).

Here are a few of my favorite books that educate, inspire, and equip you to be a stronger leader in any context:

➢ Black Faces in White Places: 10 Game-Changing Strategies to Achieve Success and Find Greatness by Jeffrey Robinson, Randal Pinkett, and Philana Patterson

➢ "Rise and Grind" by Daymond John

➢ The New Jim Crow: Mass Incarceration in the Age of Colorblindness by Michelle Alexander

➢ The Wealth Choice: Success Secrets of Black Millionaires by Dennis Kimbro

➢ Women Don't Ask: Negotiation and the Gender Divide by Linda Babcock and Sara Laschever

➢ How Exceptional Black Women Lead: Unlocking the Secrets to Creating Phenomenal Success in Career and in Life by Dr. Avis Jones-DeWeever

➢ Work It : Secrets for Success from the Boldest Women in Business by Carrie Kerpen

➢ The Power of Latino Leadership: Culture, Inclusion, and Contribution by Juana Bordas

There are so many books! Those listed will get you started.

Humanist Approach to Diversity and Resistance to Change: Jennifer Hancock

Jennifer Hancock

Founder of Humanist Learning Systems, Inc.

www.humanistlearning.com

Jennifer Hancock is a mom, author of The Bully Vaccine, and founder of Humanist Learning Systems. Jennifer is unique in that she was raised as a freethinker and is considered one of the top speakers and writers in the world of Humanism today. Her professional background is varied including stints in both the for profit and non-profit sectors. She has served as Director of Volunteer Services for the Los Angeles SPCA, sold international franchise licenses for a biotech firm, was the Manager of Acquisition Group Information for a ½ billion-dollar company and served as the executive director for the Humanists of Florida. When she became a mother, she decided to stay at home. But that didn't last long. Shortly after her son was born, she published her first book, The Humanist Approach to Happiness: Practical Wisdom. Her speaking and teaching business coalesced into the founding of Humanist Learning Systems which provides online personal and professional development training in humanistic business management and science-based harassment training that actually works. Jennifer teaches humanist management and how to use behavioral science to stop harassment, bullying, and more. Both are at play when we are dealing with diversity issues.

I asked Jennifer for **ways that a leader can foster diversity, inclusion, and acceptance within their unit/department/organization**. She responded with passion:

"Leaders and teams need a variety of inter-related skills to help ensure diversity is achieved. First, a leader must Understanding the value that diversity brings to the team (which is better problem solving) REALLY -

BETTER PROBLEM SOLVING!!! They must possess a philosophical under-standing of how to cope and change their thinking about other people so that they don't respond negatively – or if they do – they can work through it. [No one gets it right all the time. As Jennifer suggests, establishing a foundation of understanding and instilling the importance of diversity provides some "wiggle room" when you do not get it quite right.] *A leader wishing to foster diversity, inclusion, and acceptance must present a mis-sion focused and intentional integration of viewpoints. As long as the team remains focused on collaborative problem solving, issues with disa-greements can be resolved rationally and not devolve into tribal conflicts which then use harassment and bullying to socially exclude a rival idea. Leaders must employ behavior-based approaches to bullying and harass-ment that actually fix the problem.*

It isn't enough to say – it's illegal – don't do it. It's not enough to give people culture sensitivity trainings. Aggressive behavior happens, and such behaviors are used to socially exclude people [("others")] in order gain or maintain power and control over the group. These people and their actions a) kill diversity as the diverse viewpoints are targeted, and b) create a climate where incredibly bad decisions are made. Fixing this re-quires a behavioral understanding of how to get unwanted behaviors to stop and how to reward the pro-social behaviors you do want and most importantly – how to handle the people who resist!!!"

This is where I asked, **"How does a leader add diversity to a homogene-ous team that is also resistant to change."**

"First – everyone is resistant to change. Even people who want to change resist change. We can't help it. Resistance is instinctual. It's not a sign of people not wanting to change. It's just the process people go through to change. [In order] to help people with change, you must understand the behavioral dynamic playing out. You must understand what about the dy-namic is causing the resistance and how to help the team move through the change process quickly. [Take the time to] identity those [on the team who are] most resistant. Now isolate their "freak out" so it doesn't impact

the rest of the team.   I said this last bit in lay language. In scientific language, it means understanding that when you stop rewarding an old [undesirable] behavior, the behavior escalates as the organism tries to get their reward back. As they continue to not get their reward – their resistance escalates until their behavior – explodes – which is called an extinction burst – or blow out. The outcome is predictable. How bad it gets, that is the variable. For most people, it's not too bad. Some people – it's really bad. A cultural change process, if effective, is going to take all this science-based knowledge into account and help the not-bad people adjust quickly and identify those most resistant. So that the most resistant individuals aren't allowed to prevent the rest of the team from making progress.

The major way that people resist diversity is through harassment and bullying. So, that's where a pro-active effort is taken to protect those likely to be targeted. As a leader trying to foster diversity, makes sure those who are the likely target of harassment and bullying are protected and nurtured so they a) stay [with the team and the organization] and so that b) the resistance to their presence is unsuccessful. Yes, this takes effort – pro-active effort – conscientious effort - time and effort. Which is why – most leaders – even well-meaning leaders – fail. [I appreciate Jennifer's candor. It begs the question, to you as a new or emerging leader, "Are you willing to put in the time and effort or will you take the road most travelled?"] *For those truly dedicated to the project, it can be done. To give yourself the best chance at succeeding, you need to get training on behavioral modification techniques as they apply to organizational dynamics. This will equip you to pay special attention to how behavioral unlearning manifests in bullying and harassment situations. And yes – I have training on all of this."*

Diversity Must Include LGBT: Stan C. Kimer

Stan C. Kimer

President of Total Engagement Consulting by Kimer

www.totalengagementconsulting.com

Unlike the other experts spotlighted in this book, I am going to provide Stan C. Kimer's full bio. I do so not to make him seem more important than others (I greatly value every contributor equally), rather I want to show you the impact one person can make by instilling the importance of diversity with inclusion in the workplace.

"[L]eaders must be able to articulate the strategic importance of diversity to the organization's success." Stan C. Kimer

Bio:
Stan C. Kimer combines his passion for personal growth with world-class business know-how to propel enterprises to gain efficiencies and grow profit through total engagement. He is recognized as an internal / external consultant with unique skills in employee development / career mapping, LGBT (Lesbian, Gay, Bisexual, Transgender) diversity management and organizational effectiveness / project management. He is also acclaimed throughout the business community for his ability to lead large and small companies to achieve significant revenue from the under-served $732 Billion LGBT marketplace and to maximize performance of LGBT employees.

Stan excelled as a member of IBM's executive team in his most recent position of Director of Global Sales Operations with IBM's Consulting Practice. As the initial architect in building IBM's Global Sales Operations unit, Stan led the work to successfully consolidate 3000 IBM employees across 5 IBM Divisions and 18 geographic units. He drove the establishment of a single integrated high-performing cost-effective team, delivering both a $40M cost reduction (over 10%) and enhanced service levels. Stan then developed an innovative career mapping process that increased the Sales Operation's employee participation rate in career planning from under 20% to over 80%, transforming the team into the function with the highest employee morale of all IBM's 11 globalized service units.

Prior to the Sales Operations role, Stan had over 20 additional years of broad IBM experience in staff and management positions in customer support, finance, marketing, technical product planning and human resources (diversity). In the global corporate diversity role that Stan held for five years, he led IBM to premier leadership industry in LGBT diversity, including winning all 5 key marketplace LGBT diversity awards over his tenure. Stan is often called on to take over the most challenging areas and troubled projects and is recognized for always delivering quick turnaround results for team success.

Stan received his MBA from the University of Chicago Graduate School of Business and BS in Management Science from Georgia Tech. He is active in leadership roles in a dozen community and civic organizations including as a past President of the North Carolina Council of Churches. Stan frequently leads strategic planning and organizational effectiveness work with these non-profits, including providing diversity and leadership development seminars. The Triangle Business Journal recognized Stan with a "Leader in Diversity-Role Model" Award in 2013.

Here is what Mr. Kimer had to say when asked about the importance of diversity in the workplace:

"In terms of fostering diversity at work - first, leaders must be able to articulate the strategic importance of diversity to the organization's success. They need to communicate the strong connection between diversity and the organization's or team's vision and goals. These can include recruiting the best talent to the team, being creative with products and services, selling to diverse markets and more. Then second, the leader needs for all their team to see and understand that every single person on the team is unique and has their special set of diversity attributes. Even if the team may look

homogeneous, it is not! Every person is unique. It is important for every person to see that they are part of the diversity mix and have some special strength to bring to the table. Establish the baseline of "We," not "us and them." From that base, people appreciate their own diversity; they can be much more open to understanding and accepting others."

On his website, he gave great insight to the positive financial impact of diversity with inclusiveness:

"Companies who successfully develop and execute an LGBT Diversity Strategy can both increase revenue through winning in the $732B LGBT marketplace and increase employee productivity by providing a welcoming environment that fully engages all employees to contribute their best. The successful company will include the LGBT diversity components within a holistic corporate diversity strategy. The components to plan and execute should include an inclusive Equal Opportunity policy, Domestic Partner Benefits, LGBT-focused Sales and Marketing, LGBT community support, manager and employee training, providing assistance for gender-transitioning employees, providing for employee networks and more. In addition, non-profit groups can expand their volunteer base and improve services to their constituents through proactive LGBT diversity management."

Women in Leadership

Since we are discussing diversity and inclusion, this is a good time to consider a few thoughts on women in leadership. I purposely chose three differing views. When asked whether women make better leaders, these experts each gave their perspectives on women in leadership and women as leaders. You get to decide whose views match or contradict your own.

Sean Goodwin is a legal affairs consultant for *Joseph Farzam Law Firm* in Los Angeles, CA with a background of business management, HR and paralegal studies. WEBSITE: https://www.farzamlaw.com/

"The question of whether or not women make better leaders than men is difficult to answer because traits identified as leadership qualities in men are often mischaracterized as problematic personality traits in women. Being assertive is being "bitchy;" being professional is being "cold;" being personable is "using sex appeal to sell;" being assertive is being "pushy" and being attentive is "micromanaging." Many people are conditioned to equate female authority with mothering; thus, they resent it because of the conflation of that authority with infantilization. While women have no difference in competencies or capacity for leadership than men, the way their authority is responded to presents a significant barrier to obtaining leadership positions which men do not face."

Jamie Cunningham is a Partner at Piller Foods, distributor of local organic dry goods serving the Canadian market. As Business Coach and Advisor at SalesUp! Business Coaching, Mr. Cunningham works with those who want to grow and scale their businesses. Mr. Cunningham is the Owner of JE Properties, Inc., a company that creates joint venture partnerships that invest in residential properties and manages the portfolios of investment properties.

Mr. Cunningham has been helping business grow their companies since 2004. He led to this work after meeting numerous business owners who were working long hours and were emotional and physically exhausted from how much they had to sacrifice for the privileges and responsibilities of business ownership. Many were disillusioned by not always realizing the rewards they sought. Now, Mr.

Cunningham helps those same business owners to materialize the dreams they had when they started out on their entrepreneurial journey – to be in control of their future rather than feeling a slave to the business – to be able to grow and scale their business without losing their life and family doing it.

"Neither Women or Men are better leaders. The comparison is way to generalised (sic). There are characteristics that make great leaders which both women and men have the capacity to develop. Within the characteristics set of a great leader, there may be some that are easier for women to develop, such as empathy and some that may be easier for men, such as candid communication. That said, I've seen situations where the reverse is true.

The truth is, while everyone is a specific gender, where they actually sit on the scale of masculine and feminine traits varies dramatically. There are women who can be very masculine and men who can be very feminine. We also all have different personalities, backgrounds, beliefs and values which all contribute to how much work we need to do to become a great leader.

To become a great leader requires dedication and a healthy dose of personal development. The true defining factor in any person's ability to become a great leader is their willingness to look at themselves and put the work in to develop the traits that make a great leader"

Open to helping others, Jamie Cunningham can be reached at:

Email: jamie@salesup.com.au

Web: www.salesup.com.au

Ph: +1 226 473 1093 ext. 1

Ph: +61 499026 684

https://www.linkedin.com/in/coachjamiec/

https://www.facebook.com/SalesUpBusinessCoaching/

Yonason Goldson is director of Ethical Imperatives, LLC. He's an ethics coach, strategic storyteller, and TEDx speaker. He is also a community rabbi, recovered hitchhiker and circumnavigator, former newspaper columnist, and retired high school teacher in St. Louis, where he and his wife live happily as empty-nesters. Rabbi Goldson has authored five books, including Fix Your Broken Windows: a 12-step system for ethical affluence. Visit him at http://eth-icalimperatives.com, or contact him at info@ethicalimperatives.com

Rabbi Goldson offers his biblical perspective on whether women are better leaders.

"Biology, psychology, physiology, and sociology -- all these have something to say about a woman's place in the world. But what is the position of theology? When the Israelites entered their land after 40 years wandering in the desert, they were ruled for the next 400 years by a series of judges who served as both jurists and generals. Joshua was the first. Samuel was the last. But which of them was the greatest?

According to the sages of the Talmud, the most successful judge of all was Deborah. She displayed such impeccable wisdom that no one could argue with her decisions. She possessed extraordinary wealth, so no one suspected her of graft. She held court publicly where all could witness her proceedings, so no one questioned her integrity. She led her soldiers victoriously into battle, ushered in an era of unprecedented peace and prosperity, and inspired in her people a fervent commitment to spiritual and moral values. The sages teach that, as a rule, men are tacticians -- better able to react swiftly and act decisively under pressure. In contrast, women tend to be more strategic, recognizing nuances and long-term consequences that men easily overlook. Consequently, the sages understood that a partnership between men and women most often prospers when the man takes the lead while the woman directs from behind the scenes.

Modern society equates success with fame and adulation. But traditional Judaism sees the public role of leadership as something to be avoided whenever possible. The spotlight is an unforgiving place, one not to be sought after. However, someone has to lead, and better that a man should sacrifice his personal privacy than a woman. However, when called upon to do the job, a woman is likely to do as good a job, or better. Like Deborah."

Chapter Eleven:
Encourage and Motivate Your Followers

One of the worst developments in the workplace was the creation of the term "Human Resources." Formerly known as the "Personnel Department," the focus was on dealing with people as *persons*. At a time when industry focused (supposedly) on making the workplace more humane to increase job satisfaction and productivity, it took a major step backward.

No one wants to be considered a "human resource." A resource is something you use as long as it is functional. When the shelf life expires or is no longer as effective as it once was, you throw it away without a thought. It would be a glorious thing if every Human Resource department faded and the name Personnel made a resurgence.

Employees, workers, and followers are not robots. Human beings have intellect and emotions. Failing to deal with them on those levels will ultimately backfire. You cannot program loyalty.

Sharing Rewards

If your followers are going to share in the work, make certain they share in the rewards. If you get a bonus for a successful task, share at least a portion of it with your followers. Sharing a bonus does not have to be monetary. For instance, you can take followers out to lunch, give time off, or anything that can allow employees to share in the positive feelings and rewards of successful outcomes. More than one employee has felt betrayed by leadership when the boss gets a big bonus, and those who do all the work get nothing. You do not need to give them half or divide it all up among all your followers, but you should at least throw them a party, provide a free lunch, or give everyone a pair of movie tickets or a lottery ticket. Do something to show they did not work hard only to see you take all the credit. Leading requires a focus on "we" not "I." Sharing rewards provides of sense of ownership in the successful completions and achievements and decreases the likelihood of loss, theft, fraud, and high turnover related to disgruntled employees. Not to mention the impact low morale can have on productivity.

Celebrating Accomplishments

Set both personal and team goals and milestones. Nothing motivates someone like public recognition. Although some may seem somewhat embarrassed by a public display, inside they have a sense of pride connected to the recognition. There has never been a recorded study that quotes an employee who was honored in public with them saying that they never wanted that to happen again. Celebrate team milestones as well. It breaks up the routine of the workday, gives a well-deserved break, and motivates people to work harder when they return to work refreshed.

Making Celebration Part of Your Culture

You do not need to decorate the office each day or have morning pep rallies, but employees should never dread the workplace. People spend most of their waking lives at work, with substantially less time for family, friends, and activities they would much rather be doing. By the very definition, they come to "work," and you have to pay them to be there. People have to feel motivated by more than just a paycheck.

Be sure to have a welcoming environment where people feel respected. Celebrate special occasions to break up the routine, but do not make celebration itself the routine of no work will get done.

Practical Illustration

Eric's team worked all quarter, sometimes pulling late nights, to meet all their metrics and goals. Eric's supervisors saw this, and they rewarded him with a bonus for a job well done as a leader. Eric was proud of himself, but he was equally proud of his staff. While it was not necessary to split the bonus with all his employees, he did come up with a way to reward them for their hard work.

Eric called his team together and said, "I'd like to announce that this quarter we did not just meet our goals. We exceeded them! Because we all did such a fantastic job, I'm having lunch catered on Friday in our favorite place. Do not bring lunch from home. Just bring your appetites!"

Eric made sure not to plan anything pressing or important that day so that his employees could celebrate and enjoy a job well done.

The country is full of good coaches. What it takes to win is a bunch of interested players.

Don Coryell

Good Leadership is Not a Mystery: Dr. Joyce Mikal-Flynn

Joyce Mikal-Flynn Ed.D., RN, FNP, MSN

Founder and CEO of Metahab.com

metahab.com

Joyce Mikal-Flynn Ed.D., RN, FNP, MSN is Professor at the School of Nursing - California State University, Sacramento, CA where she teaches undergraduate and graduate leadership. She holds a doctorate in Educational Leadership. Other than being a former Director of Nursing in several programs, Dr. Mikal-Flynn is the Founder and CEO of Metahab.com. mikalfly@csus.edu

"Clear ideas and practices on good leadership is (sic) essential. Many times, we study bad leaders, looking at what is wrong, criticizing their characteristics and practices. It is more effective to study good leaders, identifying positive features, ideals and practices. It is not a mystery as to what makes a good leader, it is more of a mystery as to why leaders do not follow the advice and practices of successful ones. Quite simply a good and effective leader first leads themselves. They take time to review how they are doing, take care of their needs, balance their lifestyle so they inspire and guide others to do so. They are disciplined and challenge themselves modeling this behavior for others. They work to better those they lead taking time to listen and learn from them. Once leaders guide others, they trust - they do not micromanage. It not essential that leaders know how to do each person's job. Good leaders spend time asking what they can do to make each person's job better, easier and more efficient, allowing employees a sense of control, mastery and creativity in their work and life.

Good leaders are friendly with employees; they just cannot be their friends. Leaders have to make tough, unpopular choices so being too friendly may hinder this responsibility. Being cordial allows for team work and an openness for employees to make comments and express ideas, but decisions must ultimately be made. They don't surprise employees with dictates. Good leaders recog-

nize the preparation for and inclusion of employee input which allows for less anxiety and frustration when changes are made and communicated.

Finally, problems occur but they are handled with respect and with the idea that problems and mistakes are opportunities for growth and development of the leader, the employee and the company."

Chapter Twelve:
Influencing Your Followers

The best leaders influence others to do something and think it was all their idea. Do not worry about taking credit for every good thing that happens on your watch. As the leader, you get credit whenever your followers succeed because you created the environment that allowed their success.

There are many who still think that people followed blindly. I do not agree. Most followers are fully aware of potential harm and consequences – as with the "teachers" in the Maslow experiments – but choose to ignore the potential consequences trusting that their leader has a grand purpose or plan. The desire to please the leader and the fear of retaliation for not following the wishes (or perceived wishes) of the leader creates a context that becomes a breeding ground for fraud, corruption, embezzlement, and poor decision-making.

The need to be a good follower may usurp or at least contradict our sense of morality, civility, and personal value system. Instead, followers take on the ethical and moral beliefs (or perceived) as their own in order to dull the pain for self-loathing and self-blame. They were doing what they were told, allowing them to push aside blaming, saying, "it was not my fault." If followers are blind, it is because they are more comfortable in the dark. While one must take responsibility for one's own actions, I do not intend or suggest overlooking the affect negative leadership can have on a follower (Gooty, 2010).

As you seek to influence your followers, re-assess your motives. You do not want them to follow you just because you are the leader. Your followers must make an informed decision to follow you, perpetually selecting you as their leader each day and with every decision. Your influence is a catalyst for change.

The Art of Persuasion

Aristotle was a master of the art persuasion, and he outlines his thinking in his work, Rhetoric, where he identifies three important factors: ethos, pathos, and logos.

- **Ethos** (credibility) persuades people using character. If you are respectful and honest, people will be more likely to follow you because of your character. Your character convinces the follower that you are someone who is worth listening to for advice.

- **Pathos** (emotional) persuades people by appealing to their emotions. For example, when a politician wants to gain support for the bill, it inevitably is argued, "it's for the children!" Babies, puppies, and kitties abound in advertising for a reason. Although a car is neither male nor female, they are sometimes called "sexy" in car commercials. Pathos allows you to tap into emotional triggers that will capture a person's attention and enlist their support, but it can be easily abused, leading to a loss of Ethos, as described above.

- **Logos** (logical) persuades people by appealing to their intellect. This approach was one of Aristotle's favorite and his forte'. Keep in mind that not everyone reacts on a rational level.

Of the three, Ethos must always come first. Ideally, you want to appeal to Pathos, back your arguments up with Logos, and never lose Ethos. President Bill Clinton appealed to people using Pathos, often saying, "I feel your pain," but there were serious questions raised about his Ethos, and he often did not back up his appeals with Logos. There is no doubt that he was successful, but there is also no doubt that he was not as successful as he could have been.

The Principles of Influence

Robert B. Cialdini, Ph. D. once said, "It is through the influence process that we generate and manage change." In his studies, he outlined five universal principles of influence, which are useful and effective in a wide range of circumstances.

Reciprocation: People are more willing to do something for you if you have already done something for them first. Married couples do this all the time, giving in on little things so they can ask for that big night out or a chance to watch the game later.

Commitment: You cannot get people to commit to you or your vision if they do not see your commitment. Once you provide a solid, consistent example, they will feel they have to do the same.

Authority: If people believe you know what you are talking about and accept your expertise, they are far more likely to follow you. Despite the rebel cry, "Question Authority," when people need help with something, they will seek out an authority figure. If you place a man in a tie next to a man in jeans and a ratty T-shirt, people will invariably ask the man in the tie for advice on a technical subject first simply because he *looks* like an authority.

Social Validation: As independent as we like to consider ourselves, we love to be part of a crowd. It will always be a part of us; that child-like (almost innocent) desire to be accepted, no matter how many times our parents tell us, "If everyone jumped off a cliff, would you join them?" People will always jump on the bandwagon if their friends like the band.

Friendship: People listen to their friends. If they know you and like you, they are far more likely to support you. A pleasant personality can make up for a multitude of failures. It is not uncommon for a group to abandon a leader at the first sign of trouble, especially if the leader is not very well liked.

CREATING AN IMPACT

As mentioned before, communication is more than just words. There are many forms of communication, and an effective leader needs to master and know when to use them. The more of the previous leadership skills you develop, the more of an impact you will make. Additionally, the bigger the impact, the greater the positive change you can create.

Impact is created by several intangible factors, a strong and confident:

- ability to communicate, tempered by the ability to listen

- bearing, tempered by a kindly manner

- commitment to innovation, tempered by situational reality

- commitment to your followers, tempered by the ability to lead

- insistence on following the rules, tempered by flexibility

- intellect, tempered by the willingness to learn

- sense of emotion, tempered by self-control

- sense of justice, tempered by mercy

Above all: maintain a strong personal commitment to your vision.

Practical Illustration

Sarah was nervous about going to see her boss, Robyn, about a request. Robyn was stern, strict, and always carried an air of authority. Sarah lightly knocked on Robyn's door, and she invited Sarah inside.

After some small talk, Sarah cut to the chase. "Robyn, the reason I came to see you today is that I think that our client would benefit from holding our next meeting at a more casual location. I know the rule is that we go to business offices, hotels, and other professional places; however, I could see this particular client being more suited to a casual, friendly dining spot. I think it would have a positive influence on the sale."

Robyn listened and then said, "It looks like you've given this a lot of thought. Follow through with the idea, Sarah."

She was surprised. "Really? Thanks!"

While Robyn was a strict authority figure by nature, she also knew when to be flexible to the rules.

Good plans shape good decisions. That's why good planning helps to make elusive dreams come true.

Lester R. Bittel

No One Wants to be the 'Grim Reaper': Kristin Halpin Perry

Kristin Halpin Perry

Founder and Chief Consultant-in-Arms

Veraz Consulting

verazconsulting.com

kristin@verazconsulting.com

"The first step is acknowledging to yourself that your leadership style isn't working." - Kristin Halpin Perry

"I have found that the first step is the most difficult because many people believe that acknowledging there is an issue is a sign of weakness. Not true. In fact, it's quite the opposite. No matter how long someone has been a leader, there is always something to learn and develop. Life is full. Generations are changing the way we see things. Business is shifting how we operate. Technology is leading us down a path of excitement coupled with confusion and constant unknown. Without evolution, we will become stagnant. Leadership operates the same way. Leaders need to evolve and develop with the changing times. It's how we gain wisdom and knowledge and set examples for the next generation.

The second step is looking within rather than pointing the finger at others. If leadership is the right path for you, invest in yourself. Work with a mentor or an executive coach. Take a leadership course to better understand your strengths and areas of development. Everybody has them. Ask for help. This demonstrates courage and fortitude.

The third step is to embrace the feedback. I've seen poor leaders resist valuable information about themselves because of fear or ego. It doesn't work. The issues will continue to surface one way or the other and often times results in a continuous spiral down a dark path. Model good leadership. Show that learning and development is what makes leaders strong and well respected.

I worked closely with a talented operations leader who exceeded expectations from a deliverable perspective. His numbers were off the charts, which made the CFO and CEO very happy. The challenge he faced was that he had a team that didn't respect him because of the way he treated them. They described his leadership style as demeaning, demoralizing and shameful. He had the highest turnover of any leader in the company and had a reputation as being the "Grim Reaper".

After multiple complaints to the CEO and to HR, they decided to hire an Executive Coach to conduct a 360 review. The review resulted in honest, yet difficult feedback for the Head of Operations. He was stunned by the criticism because he based his leadership success on the numbers, not on how he led and supported his team. His blind spot was his inability to be in tune with his people and his overall emotional intelligence (EQ). The executive coach worked with him for several months on understanding the behavioral attributes and how to modify his leadership style moving forward. Although the path was difficult, he embraced the feedback and completely turned his leadership style and reputation around to become one of the most transformed leaders I've ever worked with."

No More Secret Squirrels: John Barker

John Barker

CEO of Attolo Systems

jbarker@attollosystems.com

www.attollosystems.com

John Barker has 20 years providing technology consulting providing outsource Chief Information Officer services and leading-edge cybersecurity tools with his company Attollo Systems. John has earned a bachelor's degree in business administration and an MBA both with concentrations in management. John writes a monthly technology column for InsideNova.com and the Culpeper Times. He has earned a variety of technical and business certifications including, PMP, ITILv3, Lean Six Sigma, & Microsoft Certified Systems Administration. John also earned his private pilot's certificate in 2008.

"Change is stressful. Not knowing if the outcome of change will be better than the current situation is the primary reason many people avoid it. It's truly the fear of the unknown.

If a company is going to make significant changes it is important to keep staff informed if not somewhat involved during the process. The absolute worst thing a leader can do is spring planned changes on unsuspecting staff members at the exact moment a change needs to occur. This goes double if the change is not expected to be popular.

Changes in company environments are very similar to the 5 stages of grief. Staff will go thru denial, anger, bargaining, depression, and finally acceptance. The earlier a planned change can begin to get communicated to the team members, the earlier they can begin dealing with it. This stretches out the time that staff have to cope and plan themselves for what's on the horizon. It will not be as an abrupt situation.

Leaders that don't communicate potential change until it must be implemented will be met with massive amounts of resistance and should expect productivity to take a nosedive. Leaders will be dealing with everyone going thru the 5 stages of grief in a compressed time frame but still expect them perform. This is naive assumption on the leader's part.

As a leader it's important to communicate the good and the bad. Change is inevitable. Show your staff respect and keep them informed on upcoming changes. They will trust you more and probably thank you in the end."

Chapter Thirteen:
Realistic and S.M.A.R.T. Goals

A vision without specific, targeted goals is just a wish or a hope. Without targeted goals, how will you ever know if your vision is being accomplished? A vision needs a project roadmap with milestones, but how do you determine what those goals are? First, we will discuss goals themselves, then how to determine what your goals should be and how to support them.

Setting S.M.A.R.T. Goals

S.M.A.R.T. goals are:

- **Specific:** The vision itself is general while the goals are specific targets to be met. Specific goals answer the questions of who, what, when, where, why, and how questions as specifically as possible.

- **Measurable***:* Goals must be measurable - progress and attainment. They must be tracked according to the amount of time or money spent, or results achieved as appropriate.

- **Attainable***:* A goal which cannot be met, is not a goal, it is an ideal. If you know you need certain infrastructure in place to accomplish your vision, you should break down your goals into attainable steps you can monitor as each step is put into place.

- **Realistic***:* A goal may be attainable, but not with the resources at hand. In that case, you need other goals to build up to the level where the attainable goal becomes realizable. A goal may be possible, but you need the right people with the right amount of time and support to make it happen.

- **Timed**: All goals need to be accomplished within a given time frame. Deadlines may indeed be missed, but without any time-table, there will be no sense of urgency and no reason not to put it off until "later."

Each goal should lead to the "next step" in the overall plan until the ultimate vision is reached.

Creating a Long-Term (Strategic) Plan

Also called Strategic Planning, the long-term plan is the road map that guides you to the ultimate realization of your vision. As discussed in the previous Chapter, the goal may be possible, but not attainable or realistic now. You may be missing a quality person for a key position, you may lack the funds, or time to achieve the higher-level goals, so lower level stepping stone goals must be planned. Strategy is necessary to set, communicate, and meet goals. Strategy and vision work together to shape or reshape the context. One can have a vision without a strategy, but cannot create a strategy without a vision. Strategy, I think, is one of the first steps in transitioning a vision into reality.

If your goal is to unify a modern computer network throughout your organization, but you only have a few outdated computers and older shared printers, your ultimate goal will be possible and attainable, but not realistic. If you do not have the money for the new equipment and do not have a strong IT person on staff, your goal will be unattainable. If you need everything done in a week, your goal cannot be timely, as it will take much longer. Intermediate goals, however, can make your ultimate goal realistic, attainable, and timely.

You might first want to increase your revenue through increased sales, a fundraiser, long-term business loan, or by other means. You can make a goal to hire a network guru for a reasonable cost who can analyze your current systems and determine what needs to be upgraded according to modern networking technology. That analysis will provide you the information to set new goals of buying, configuring, and implementing the equipment, then adding the infrastructure to network it all together. In the end, the goal that seemed impossible will become a reality, according to your original vision.

Creating a Support System

Once your goals are established, you need a way to ensure they are set into motion. Duties must be assigned, and documentation must be established to support and track progress. A Gantt Chart is a great way to track milestones over a period of time. You need to establish the tools necessary to track progress or development as appropriate. These might include a simple checklist for some tasks and complicated advanced software tracking systems for others.

Monitoring and oversight are the keys to achieving all goals. A good leader realizes that the leader cannot do everything. Well, if the leader is capable, they should not do so. Let's go back to the discussion on shared vision. Shared vision requires shared responsibility for bringing the vision to fruition. If the employees, your followers, are not involved, then how can they share in the vision, in the experience. You delegate not because you do not feel like doing the work. Delegate because you want to support the growth, creativity, and leadership abilities of your followers.

Gantt Chart Example retrieved from https://www.teamgantt.com/

Practical Illustration

Sophie presented her goals to Thomas, the leader, and she said, "What do you think of the plan that we have laid out?"

Thomas said, "I think that your goal of updating our technology is specific, measurable, attainable, and timed. However, the only thing that is unrealistic about the goal is how much it is going to cost."

Sophie said, "I was hoping that you could help me brainstorm ways to come up with the revenue."

Thomas nodded. "In the past, we've tried new ways of increasing sales to pay for equipment that we needed, or taken out a business loan. But given the time frame, I feel like our best bet is a fundraiser."

They included the fundraiser idea in the final goal, making sure once again that the goal was

SMART:

Specific, Measurable, Attainable, Realistic, and Time anchored.

Chapter Fourteen
The End is Just the Beginning

To be a leader, you must first see yourself as a leader. Based on what you have learned so far, you now know what qualities are important in a leader and you have prioritized them as they apply to you. Experience is the greatest teacher, however, and there is no substitute. If you ever had a boss that infuriated you and made you want to quit your job, you know what not to do. If you ever had a parent, teacher, coach, or supervisor who inspired you, you have a good example to follow.

Here are three things to remember as to take the next steps in your life and career:

1. There is no better time than the present to emerge as a leader. You are necessary!

2. You are a leader even if you are only leading yourself. Do that well! After all, how can you expect anyone else to follow you if you cannot or will not follow yourself? Meaning, if you cannot exhibit self-control and self-respect, then why would anyone allow you to have even the slightest control over their lives or career? Why would they respect you? Okay, so there is an exception to every rule. Just do not sit and bank on you being the exception – Instead, be exceptional!

3. Proceed in excellence. As I said in my book, *I AM MORE Surviving Survival*, "Excellence is doing what is right, in the right manner, at the right time, for the right reason, with the right attitude, in a way that will produce the greatest positive impact." A reason, for the sake of this concept, is simply a statement of your circumstance. An excuse is a blockage (situation, character

flaw, lack) you allow to prevent you from overcoming a circumstance.

It was hard trying to decide what to include in this book. There is so much to learn about leadership. I reminded myself that there are a plethora of books on leadership and my goal was to introduce the fundamental of leadership and influence for new and emerging leaders. The task I set before myself was simple – why complicate it? So, no, this book is not all encompassing. You do need to continue to train, read, research, and shadow other leaders. You will experience struggles, failure, and unnerving moments; however, knowing the fundamentals will give you a foundation necessary to confidently pull yourself together and lead on. I trust your triumphs and positive organizational and social impact will far exceed any difficult times.

Leadership is a difficult role – whether leading from the front, from within, or from behind. You are born for this!

References

Algera, P. & Lips-Wiersma, M. (2012) Radical authentic leadership: Co-creating the conditions under which all members of the organization can be authentic. The Leadership Quarterly, 23, pp. 118-131.

Bennis, W. (2009). On becoming a leader (4th edition). New York, NY: Basic Books. LP 762 The Psychology of Leadership and Followership Dr. Dan Jacobs Fall Semester 2016 3

Black, D. (1976). The behavior of law. New York: Academic Press.

Brunson, R. K. (2005). Young Black Men and Urban Policing in the United States. British Journal of Criminology, 46(4), 613-640. doi:10.1093/bjc/azi093

Burns, J.M. (1978). Leadership. New York, NY: HarperPerennial.

Can, A. & Aktas, M. (2012). Cultural values and followership style preferences. Procedia-Social and Behavioral Sciences, 41, 84-91.

Carsten, M., Uhl-Bien, M., West, B., Patera, J. & McGregor, R. (2010). Exploring social constructions of followership: A qualitative study. The Leadership Quarterly, 21, pp. 543-562.

Chatman, J. & Kennedy, J., Psychological perspectives on leadership, pp. 159-174.

Coates, T.-N. (2015). Between the world and me: Notes on the First 150 years in America. New York, NY, United States: Random House.

Collins, J. (2001). Good to great: Why some companies make the leap...and others don't. New York, NY: HarperBusiness.

Dansereau, F., Seitz, S., Chiu, C., Shaughnessy, B. & Yammarino, F. (2013). What makes leadership, leadership? Using self-expansion theory to integrate traditional and contemporary approaches. The Leadership Quarterly, 24, pp. 798-821.

Dinh, J., Lord, R., Gardner, W., Meuser, J., Liden, R. & Hu, J. (2014). Leadership theory and research in the new millennium: Current theoretical trends and changing perspectives. The Leadership Quarterly, 25, pp. 33-62.

Eberly, M., Johnson, M., Hernandez, M. & Avolio, B. (2013). An integrative process model of leadership: Examining loci, mechanisms, and event cycles. American Psychologist, 68 (6), pp. 427-443.

Fairhurst, G. & Connaughton, S. (2014). Leadership: A communicative perspective. Leadership, 10 (1), pp. 7-35.

Fairhurst, G. & Uhl-Bien, M. (2012). Organizational discourse analysis (ODA): Examining leadership as a relational process. The Leadership Quarterly, 23, pp. 1043-1062.

Faris, N. & Parry, K. (2011). Islamic organizational leadership within a Western society: The problematic role of external context. The Leadership Quarterly, 22, pp. 132-151.

Ganz, M., Leading Change: Leadership, organization, and social movements, pp. 527-561.

Gardner, W., Cogliser, C., Davis, K. & Dickens, M. (2011). Authentic leadership: A review of the literature and research agenda. The Leadership Quarterly, 22, pp. 1120-1145.

Gooty, J., Connelly, S., Griffity, J. & Gupta, A. (2010). Leadership affect and emotions: A state of the science review. The Leadership Quarterly, 21, pp. 979-1004.

Graen, G. & Uhl-Bien, M. (1995). Development of leader-member exchange (LMX) theory of

Haslam, S.A., et al. (2015). 'Happy to have been of service': The Yale archive as a window into the engaged followership of participants in Milgram's 'obedience' experiments. British Journal of Social Psychology, 54, p. 55-83.

Hernandez, M., Eberly, M., Avolio, B. & Johnson, M. (2011). The loci and mechanisms of leadership: Exploring a more comprehensive view of leadership theory. The Leadership Quarterly, 22, pp. 1165-1185.

Hill, L. A., et al., Unlocking the slices of genius in your organization: Leading for innovation, pp. 611-646.

Hinojosa, A., McCauley, K., Randolph-Seng, B. & Gardner, W. (2014). Leaders and follower attachment styles: Implications for authentic leader-follower relationships. The Leadership Quarterly, 25, pp. 595-610.

http://www.managementtoday.co.uk/article/1385889

Huetterman, H., Doering, S. & Boerner, S. (2014). Leadership and team identification: Exploring the followers' perspective. The Leadership Quarterly, 25, pp. 413-432.

Ibarra, H., Snook, S., & Guillen Ramo, L., Identity-based leader development, pp. 657-674.

Jacqueline Novogratz: "Inspiring a life of immersion" (video, 19:46 minutes): https://youtu.be/jbHpF7Ey_ck

Javidan, M., et al., Leadership and Cultural Context: A theoretical and empirical examination based on project GLOBE, pp. 335-372.

Jones, G. & Spooner, C. (2006). Coaching high achievers. Consulting Psychology Journal: Practice and Research, 58 (1), pp. 40-50.

Junker, N. & van Dick, R. (2014). Implicit theories in organizational settings: A systematic review and research agenda of implicit leadership and followership theories. The Leadership Quarterly, 25, pp. 1154-1173.

Kegan, R. & Lahey, L., Adult development and organizational leadership, pp. 769-787.

Kellerman, B. (2012). The end of leadership. New York, NY: HarperBusiness.

Kim, C. & Schachter, H. (2015). Exploring followership in a public setting: Is it a missing link between participative leadership and organizational performance? American Review of Public Administration, 45 (4), pp. 436-457.

Laustsen, L. & Petersen, M. (2015). Does a competent leader make a good friend? Conflict, ideology and the psychologies of friendship and followership. Evolution and Human Behavior, 36, p. 286-293.

Liden, R. & Antonakis, J. (2009). Considering context in psychological leadership research. Human Relations, 62 (11), pp. 1587-1605.

Lorsch, J., A Contingency Theory of Leadership, pp. 411-428.

Luthans, F. (2010). Organizational behavior (12th edition). Boston, MA: McGraw-Hill Irwin.

Malakyan, P. (2014). Followership in leadership studies: A case of leader-follower trade approach. Journal of Leadership Studies, 7 (4), pp. 6-22.

May, D., Wesche, J., Heinitz, K. & Kerschreiter, R. (2014). Coping with destructive leadership: Putting forward an integrated theoretical framework for the interaction process between leaders and followers. Zeitschrift fur Psychologie, 222 (4), pp. 203-213.

Michael Useem of the Wharton School, McKinsey Quarterly video interview with Bill Javetski from August 2012 (video, 6:31 minutes): http://www.mckinsey.com/insights/leading_in_the_21st_century/an_interview_with_michael_useem

Monzani, L, Ripoll, P. & Peiro, J. (2015). Winning the hearts and minds of followers: The interactive effects of followers' emotional competencies and goal setting types of trust in leadership. Revista Latinoamericana de Psicologia, 47 (1), pp. 1-15.

Mustafa, G. & Lines, R. (2014). Influence of leadership on job satisfaction: The moderating effects of follower individual-level masculinity-femininity values. Journal of Leadership Studies, 7 (4), pp. 23- 39.

Nye, Joseph S., Power and Leadership, pp. 305-327.

Oc, B. & Bashur, M. (2013). Followership, leadership and social influence. The Leadership Quarterly, 24, pp. 919-934.

Olafur Eliasson & Frederik Ottesen's MIT Talk: "Turning ideas into action" from 2014 (video, 78 minutes): http://video.mit.edu/watch/olafur-eliasson-at-mit-turning-ideas-into-action-27703/

Podolny, J., Khurana, R., & Besharov, M., Revisiting the Meaning of Leadership, pp. 65-100.

Polsfuss, C. & Ardichvili, A. (2008). Three principles psychology: Applications in leadership development and coaching. Advances in Developing Human Resources, 10 (5), pp. 671-685. LP 762 The Psychology of Leadership and Followership Dr. Dan Jacobs Fall Semester 2016 5

Popper, M. (2013). Leaders perceived as distant and close: Some implications for psychological theory on leadership. The Leadership Quarterly, 24, pp. 1-8.

Ricardo Semler's MIT Talk: "Leading by omission" from September 2005 (video, 48 minutes): https://www.youtube.com/watch?v=JJ0FQR2gXe0 LP 762 The Psychology of Leadership and Followership Dr. Dan Jacobs Fall Semester 2016 6

Roselinde Torres' TED Talk: "What it takes to be a great leader" from October 2013 (video, 9 minutes): http://www.ted.com/talks/roselinde_torres_what_it_takes_to_be_a_great_leader?language=en#t-9514

Schein, E. H. (2011). Helping: How to offer, give, and receive help. San Francisco: Berrett-Koehler Publishers.

Sharma, P. & Kirkman, B. (2015). Leveraging leaders: A literature review and future lines of inquiry for empowering leadership research. Group & Organization Management, 40 (2), pp. 193-237.

Stanley Milgram Obedience Experiment (1962) video at: https://youtu.be/1HcMWlnTtFQ

Steffens, N., Haslam, S.A., Reicher, S., Platow, M., Fransen, K., Yang, J., Ryan, M., Jetten, J., Peters, K. & Boen, F. (2014). Leadership as social identity management: Introducing the Identity Leadership Inventory (ILI) to assess and validate a four-dimensional model. The Leadership Quarterly, 25, pp. 1001-1024.

Sy, T. (2010). What do you think of followers? Examining the content, structure, and consequences of implicit followership theories. Organizational Behavior and Human Decision Processes, 113, pp. 73-84.

Tee, E., Paulsen, N. & Ashkanasy, N. (2013). Revisiting followership through a social identity perspective: The role of collective follower emotion and action. The Leadership Quarterly, 24 (6), pp. 902-918.

Thoroughgood, C., Padilla, A., Hunter, S. & Tate, B. (2012). The susceptible circle: A taxonomy of followers associated with destructive leadership. The Leadership Quarterly, 23, pp. 897-917.

Uhl-Bien, M., Riggio, R., Lowe, K. & Carsten, M. (2014). Followership theory

Ursula M. Burns' MIT Talk: "A conversation on leadership" from 3/3/11 (video, 64 minutes): http://video.mit.edu/watch/a-conversation-on-leadership-9657/

Wageman, R. & Hackman, R., What makes teams of leaders leadable? pp. 475-522.

About the Author

Dr. Tonisha M. Pinckney, Founder of Revelatus Specialized Accounting and Consulting, LLC, I AM MORE, LLC, and I AM MORE Institute for Excellence and Social Responsibility, Inc., is a native of Newark, NJ and is dedicated to education and advocacy. With a wide range of expertise, supported by over 16 years of experience. She is also a part-time Lecturer at Lasell College.

As a practitioner, Dr. Pinckney works with small to moderate sized businesses, religious institutions and non-profits, attorneys, and others. Service offerings include mediation, expert witness reports and testimony, risk assessment and mitigation, safe hiring, and training employees and managers. She is passionate about educating small businesses and minority communities about identity theft, fraud prevention, entrepreneurialism, non-profit sustainability, and more.

Dr. Pinckney earned a Doctor of Philosophy in Criminal Justice and Criminology (2014), a Master of Science in Criminal Justice from the University of Cincinnati (2010), and graduate certificates in Security Studies (2011) and Forensic Criminology (2012), both from the University of Massachusetts Lowell. Dr. Pinckney earned her Bachelor of Science in Accounting (2007) from Kean University in New Jersey. She is a member of the Association of Certified Fraud Examiners (ACFE) and earned the related certification. She is also a Master Analyst in Financial Forensics as earned and granted by the National Association of Certified Value Analysts (NACVA). At the NACVA she serves on the Ethics Oversight Board, an elected position. She also has a host of other educational and professional development certifications and accomplishments related to sexual offending and recidivism, expert witness testimony, emergency management, and risk assessment.

She is the President of the Board of Trustees at Worcester Recovery Center and Hospital, a Massachusetts Depart of Mental Health run institution. She is an elected member of the Board of Directors of the National Alliance on Mental Illness of Massachusetts, Inc. where she works with local law enforcement as a Crisis Intervention Team Instructor and Diversity Liaison. And, Dr. Pinckney serves on the Massachusetts Domestic and Sexual Violence Council.

Most recently, Dr. Pinckney was the Director of Criminal Justice Undergraduate and Graduate Programs at Anna Maria College in Paxton, MA. Previously, Dr. Pinckney was the Assistant Dean of Adult & Professional Studies, Online Learning, Institutional Partnership at Newbury College in Brookline. Where she was also Director of the Criminal Justice and Legal Studies Programs. Before that time, her expertise were honed as she worked in tax accounting, forensic accounting, fraud investigations, and financial analysis roles. Dr. Pinckney is an outspoken author, advocate, and activist on issues of racial, socioeconomic, and gender disparities. She helps promote and maintain diversity and inclusiveness, and advocates for more funding for mental health treatment, transportation, child mental health services, health care, and police training. She also serves as corporator, trustee, and a board member for other organizations. Fueled by her own experiences, she authored books discussing domestic violence, sexual assault, parenting, grief, mental illness, and racial and socio-economic disparity – *I AM MORE – The Journey (2009, 2016), I AM MORE: Surviving Survival (2013, 2017)*, and *Get Over It? I'm Still Going Through it! 15 Tools to Use When Going Through Tough Times (2017)*. Recognizing the importance of saying, "I AM MORE!" Dr. Pinckney registered it as a trademark. She is also the author of *My turn To Lead: Fundamentals of Leadership & Influence for New and Emerging Leaders (2018)*.

Her greatest joy is being a mother to her two college-aged sons who live life passionately as they promote positive self-image, unity, and awareness. Dr. Pinckney spends her free time laughing with family and friends, writing poetry, cooking, playing video games, watching movies, experiencing escape rooms, laser tag, and playing with the family dog.

Dr. Pinckney is available for speaking engagements, workshops, training, conferences, and freelance writing.

www.tonishapinckney.com

www.revelatusconsulting.com

www.declareiammore.com

info@revelatusconsulting.com

ask@declareiammore.com

www.ingramcontent.com/pod-product-compliance
Lightning Source LLC
Chambersburg PA
CBHW031944190326
41519CB00007B/659